The Middle Ages

A Captivating Guide to the History of Europe, Starting from the Fall of the Western Roman Empire Through the Black Death to the Beginning of the Renaissance

© **Copyright 2019**

All Rights Reserved. No part of this book may be reproduced in any form without permission in writing from the author. Reviewers may quote brief passages in reviews.

Disclaimer: No part of this publication may be reproduced or transmitted in any form or by any means, mechanical or electronic, including photocopying or recording, or by any information storage and retrieval system, or transmitted by email without permission in writing from the publisher.

While all attempts have been made to verify the information provided in this publication, neither the author nor the publisher assumes any responsibility for errors, omissions or contrary interpretations of the subject matter herein.

This book is for entertainment purposes only. The views expressed are those of the author alone, and should not be taken as expert instruction or commands. The reader is responsible for his or her own actions.

Adherence to all applicable laws and regulations, including international, federal, state and local laws governing professional licensing, business practices, advertising and all other aspects of doing business in the US, Canada, UK or any other jurisdiction is the sole responsibility of the purchaser or reader.

Neither the author nor the publisher assumes any responsibility or liability whatsoever on the behalf of the purchaser or reader of these materials. Any perceived slight of any individual or organization is purely unintentional.

Free Bonus from Captivating History (Available for a Limited time)

Hi History Lovers!

Now you have a chance to join our exclusive history list so you can get your first history ebook for free as well as discounts and a potential to get more history books for free! Simply visit the link below to join.

Captivatinghistory.com/ebook

Also, make sure to follow us on Facebook, Twitter and Youtube by searching for Captivating History.

Contents

INTRODUCTION 1

CHAPTER 1 – FALL OF THE WESTERN ROMAN EMPIRE 5

CHAPTER 2 – STEWARDS OF THE FUTURE – THE RISE OF THE BYZANTINE EMPIRE 13

CHAPTER 3 – RECLAIMING SPAIN AND EXPANDING ONE OF THE STRONGEST AND EARLIEST KINGDOMS OF THE MIDDLE AGES ... 20

CHAPTER 4 – CHARLEMAGNE – A BRIEF RETURN TO THE EMPIRE 25

CHAPTER 5 – OTTO I AND HIS NEW EMPIRE 30

CHAPTER 6 – THE GREAT SCHISM 36

CHAPTER 7 – THE FAMOUS (OR INFAMOUS) CRUSADES – 1095 TO 1291 43

CHAPTER 8 – FORGING A NEW ENGLAND 52

CHAPTER 9 – THE HUNDRED YEARS' WAR – 1337 TO 1453 63

CHAPTER 10 – THE HORRORS OF NATURE 72

CHAPTER 11 – HIGHER EDUCATION AND THE GOTHIC PERIOD – HOW THE MIDDLE AGES ADVANCED EDUCATION AND ARCHITECTURE 78

CHAPTER 12 – THE RENAISSANCE 85

CONCLUSION 90

BIBLIOGRAPHY 96

Introduction

One of the least understood periods of European history occurred between the 6th century and the 14th or 15th century (depending on which historian you ask). Commonly called the Middle Ages, this was a time period of extreme change for Europe, beginning with the fall of the Western Roman Empire. To a continent that had seen a drastic shift in the power structure, the world seemed to be particularly harsh. Rome had been a major player across Europe for well over a millennium. Then it was gone.

This is at least the impression that most people have today. The truth is far more complex and layered. Germanic tribes that had been subjugated by the Romans certainly were not upset by its fall as they again had their freedom. Nor did the Roman wealth of knowledge and understanding of the world simply disappear. Many of the people who fled Rome reached a city that would become the home to an entirely new empire. Today it is called the Byzantine Empire, but for the more than 1,000 years that the empire existed, the people considered themselves Romans.

Most of the things that people know about the Middle Ages is based on how the people who followed it wanted the previous period to be classified. The term Dark Ages likely originated during the Renaissance because the people of the time wanted to think of themselves as being so much more advanced than the people of the era that came before them. The men of the Renaissance believed they were returning to the thought processes that were lost after

Rome fell. The irony is that many of the ideas they "rediscovered" were brought back to Europe by the people of the Byzantine Empire who were fleeing *back* to Rome after their capital, Constantinople, fell. The ideas never died; they simply moved, and new thinking arose in Europe during the Middle Ages.

Some of the most famous leaders in European history lived during this time. Under leaders from Charlemagne, who fought under a Christian banner, to Otto I who would found the Ottoman Empire, the power structure began to change. Monarchs began to spawn across Europe to fill the power vacuum left by the fall of the Western Roman Empire. Perhaps the most famous (and revolutionary) power dynamics occurred in England during the 13th century. With monarchs centralizing their power throughout Europe, in England, nobles were beginning to exert their own influence, forcing their monarch to guarantee certain rights under the Magna Carta. The Hundred Years' War also consumed much of the continent as monarchs tried to take control of areas that were under the banner of other countries. The rise of two of the most notable houses in European history found influence during this time, not as rulers, but as wealthy merchants and bankers to whom religious leaders and monarchs would turn to for financial assistance.

The rise of Christianity began before Rome fell, but it was during the Middle Ages that the Church would begin to form. Nearly unrecognizable to the Catholic and Protestant Churches of today, the Christian Church during most of the Middle Ages spanned a much larger region. The power structure was spread out over cities instead of having a single location. Then, the inevitable happened toward the end of the Middle Ages—Eastern and Western Europe had different ideas about theology. The Schism was one of the more divisive times of the Middle Ages, creating the Roman Catholic Church and the Greek Orthodox Church. Both sides claimed to be Christian and derided the other for being wrong about some of their religious teachings. It was the first major break in Christianity, and it would be echoed during the early modern era with the Protestant

Reformation. Unlike the Protestant Reformation though, the Schism was far less bloody. Both sides of the Christian Church would work together to fight the Crusades against the Muslims during the Middle Ages. Civil would not be an accurate way to describe it, but the events after the Schism were more civil than what occurred after the breaking up of the Catholic Church.

Perhaps just as cruel as the wars and Crusades were the natural disasters that permanently changed Europe. The Great Famine and the Black Death remain in the collective memory of the people of Europe today because of how devastating they were. The Black Death played a key role in the transition between the Middle Ages and early modern Europe. For the first time, people began to question the Catholic Church as the members of the religious orders had proven to be just as susceptible to the ravages of the disease as the common people.

This is also a time period that still inspires art, literature, and philosophy today. There were men who lived during the Middle Ages who are still quoted and revered today, such as Saint Thomas Aquinas. They were almost always men of the cloth (religious men), but not always. People still enjoy the works of Geoffrey Chaucer, a famous writer who was also a merchant. The architecture of this time has also been used and reused for many centuries as well. The cathedrals and castles built during the Middle Ages still remain while younger structures have long since crumbled. Perhaps the most famous architecture from the time though is known as the Gothic style. The look and feel of the Gothic style have inspired many generations, including the Romantics of the 1800s and the horror/mystery genre that is still so popular today. However, it was the birth of universities that reflects the thinking of the time. Prior to the Middle Ages, there was no higher education.

Many of the institutions and ideas that the men of the Renaissance would explore began during the Middle Ages. It was a time when Europe healed from the fall of one superpower and transitioned into something that more closely resembled the map of Europe today. It would undergo many more changes in the years following the Middle Ages, but nations began to find their identities without their Roman overlords.

Chapter 1 – Fall of the Western Roman Empire

The saying goes that Rome was not built in a day, and that is absolutely true. However, it is equally true that Rome did not fall in a day. The Roman Empire had been in decline for decades—or even centuries depending on how you define the decline of an empire—and it was the rotting away of the empire that ultimately led to its end. Without the constant attacks though, the Roman Empire would probably have continued to drag on until it finally broke down on its own. The fall was inevitable, but the end of this long era of European history was an event that entirely changed the face of Europe.

Internal Decline

While the role of external forces was the obvious cause for the fall of the Western Roman Empire, it was helped along by the changes within Rome itself. Some historians point to the fall of the Roman Republic as the template that the fall of Rome would follow centuries later.

Rome had become increasingly secular and greedy, leading to leaders placing their interests over that of their country. Those in power fought with each other to gain more power after Emperor Valens died in 378 CE. Instead of working to strengthen their empire, those in power focused on fighting amongst themselves in a desperate bid to gain more power for themselves and their families. This meant that they were not interested in securing the borders or fighting off the Germanic tribes, as the Roman citizens in authority were more interested in expanding their own power within the city. Many of them likely believed that once Rome was under their control, they would be able to retake the territories that Rome had lost, not realizing that they all lacked what previous leaders had had: a dedication to Rome and its betterment.

There was also another growing problem within the city that is often overlooked—the rise of Christianity. For several centuries, Christians were used as entertainment in arenas where they would not put up a fight. What had started out as purely another spectacle ended up changing the way many people would think. The dedication of the Christians' belief in nonviolence, even to the point of allowing themselves to be killed instead of putting up a fight, was something that Romans began to find inspiring. It attracted more followers who were ready to believe in something outside of themselves, something that the people in power lacked.

The effect of Christians on the fall of the empire is perhaps best summed up by Edward Gibbon:

> A candid but rational inquiry into the progress and establishment of Christianity may be considered as a very essential part of the history of the Roman empire. While this great body was invaded by open violence, or undermined by slow decay, a pure and humble religion greatly insinuated itself into the minds of men, grew up in silence and obscurity, derived new vigour from opposition, and finally erected the triumphant banner of the cross on the ruins of the Capital.

The very people whose deaths were treated as entertainment for the masses would eventually come to rule over most of the lands that Rome had once conquered. The ideals and values taught by Jesus would lead to the rise of Christianity all over Europe during the Middle Ages. It would also be the end of Christianity as it was originally preached. Warping the values that had gained the religion so much attention, men would turn it into a new power structure. However, while Rome was still intact, Christians remained steadfast in their beliefs, putting that above nearly all else.

Prelude to the Fall

Rome had begun its decline long before the 5th century CE. Emperors like Nero and Caligula had shown the cracks in the elite, that the rulers were growing too complacent and careless. Inequality had always been rampant, but the demise of the empire would not be because the lower classes would rise up against the Romans in power. Instead, it would be the Germanic tribes that had long fought against the Romans who would start to chip away at the crumbling empire.

Almost 100 years before Rome fell, the Romans were fighting against nomadic Germanic tribes. The farther north a Roman traveled, the less "civilized" the world would seem to them. To the north of the Roman border along the Danube-Rhine were the people Romans considered to be barbarians, the people that they never successfully conquered. Since the time of Julius Caesar, the empire had fought with these people without any definitive victory. As if to distinguish between their "civilized" version of society and the unconquered people to the north, the Romans came up with the term barbarian. It was derogatory as it was based on the Romans' thinking that the Germanic tribes sounded like they were saying "bar bar bar" when they spoke. The term was a childish attempt to make the same sounds without bothering to recognize that it was an entirely different language with its own culture. Over time, those sounds would evolve into the word barbarian. Today, the word has two different connotations. It means someone uncivilized, but it also represents something akin to the noble savage. Neither is particularly flattering or accurate, but works of fiction, such as *Conan the*

Barbarian, have helped to elevate the term to be a bit more representative of the kind of harsh life these people lived.

Some emperors would try to buy control of the barbarians by offering money for them to become part of the Roman Empire. Some emperors tried to get them to join the Romans, giving them lands to settle if they would be willing to become Roman citizens. This latter method, in particular, seems to have worked as the northern people did move south and settle. But despite becoming Roman citizens, they never really gave up their own culture. The Goths were a particularly dangerous group that Rome seemed willing to ignore as the group migrated to the northern border of the empire. The intentions of the Goths seem to have been to settle in the Roman Empire as a way of improving their own very harsh lives. Rome did not view them as a threat, despite the large numbers of Goths who migrated into the empire.

The tensions between the Romans and Goths began to mount when Rome appeared to be disinterested in hearing the requests of this large group of people. The Huns posed a particular threat to the Goths, but Rome seemed unwilling to do anything to help them. As the number of Goths grew, it became difficult to provide for them. To compound the problem, the Goths could see the corruption among the Roman officials, and the extortion for basic goods was unacceptable to the people. Though many of the Goths were Christian, their patience while awaiting permission to settle on Roman lands reached its limit. Emperor Valens delayed giving an answer as he tried to gain more information about the number of people planning to migrate, and this excessive delay compounded their sense of panic. The Huns continued to press closer to the Goths and winter neared, which meant that if they did not settle soon, they would not be able to grow their own crops. The delay from the emperor was taken poorly, and they moved into the territory without his permission. Their arrival was met by skirmishes and fighting that would grow into a five-year war.

This led to one of the most notable encounters which occurred in 378 CE at the Battle of Hadrianopolis (also known as Adrianople). The Roman Emperor Valens led a large number of men to face off against a Gothic army that was far larger than the Roman army. Not only would the Romans lose roughly two-thirds of their army (estimated at between 10,000 and 20,000 men), but the emperor himself was killed in battle, all within the span of less than 24 hours.

Peace would see the Goths becoming a part of the Roman Empire, but there remained a good bit of tension between them. Some Gothic leaders would rise up to fight against Rome, though most would try to find their own place in the empire, safe from the threats they had faced living in the north. It would be one of the Gothic leaders who had fought as a Roman commander earlier who would eventually bring the city to its knees.

As the Romans tried to recover from such a catastrophic defeat, the Germanic tribes were able to chip away at the edges of the kingdom over the next century, claiming lands for themselves. These successor kingdoms would mark the obvious decline of the empire as Rome lost territories that it had gained under so many famous military leaders. Slowly but surely, the Germanic people who fought against the Romans were reclaiming what had once been theirs.

As Rome began to lose lands, they increasingly pulled their military back from areas that they felt they no longer controlled. In Gaul and Britain, the nobles lost their estates, and without them, Roman culture nearly entirely disappeared in the two areas.

Rome Falls

The man who would bring about the end of the Western Roman Empire was a Goth (a part of the western tribes called the Visigoths) who had worked alongside other Romans. Straddling the divide between the Germanic tribe and Roman allegiance, he has a unique place in history for many reasons. Since there were many contributing factors to the fall of Rome, this man's name is not nearly as well known as it should be.

The man who would accomplish what no one before him had done for hundreds of years was called Alaric. He was many things, including a Christian. But he was also very determined and fought for what he thought was right.

Rome had promised him and his people the lands in the Balkans, and he sought to get the land and some support for his people. As the emperor remained silent on his consent, Alaric began to make further demands, including a demand that his people would be given Roman citizenship. His intention was to secure their future.

Emperor Honorius would respond with a denial of the request. Each request was met with a refusal.

Seeing no other way to have the promised fulfilled, Alaric amassed an army of Goths, former slaves, and Huns and headed to Rome. They moved over the Alps and into Italy with very little resistance. As a former Roman commander, Alaric knew how to keep an army engaged and organized, making him an incredibly formidable opponent. Emperor Honorius was an incompetent emperor who focused on himself instead of the empire, and his military prowess was nonexistent. As Alaric and his army neared the city, the emperor was safely housed in his own villa in Ravenna, outside of Rome. He failed to understand the threat posed by the formidable adversary and largely continued to ignore the requests, even as the army neared the city.

Alaric did not attack the city in the early days. Instead, he had his army camp outside of Rome, blocking any goods from entering or exiting the capital. His army was unaffected (they could take whatever goods were meant to go into the city), but the Romans were not so fortunate. Without food and water, the city became weak. The man who wanted only what had been promised to him and his people would enter Rome as its conqueror in 410 CE. Alaric and his army would only remain in the city for three days, but by the time they left, they had entirely sacked the city. As a Christian, he did not allow the basilicas of St. Paul and St. Peter's to be touched by his army.

Emperor Honorius would send 6,000 soldiers to try to defend the city, but they were no match for Alaric and his men.

This led to many people seeing this as a sign from the gods or Christian god. Those who believed in the Roman gods saw it as a sign that they had failed. Christians, such as St. Augustine, would say that it was a reminder from their god that humans were flawed and that suffering was a part of their god's plan.

Rome would limp along for about another half century, with the power struggles and economic decay finally reaching its inevitable destination in 476. The last Roman emperor was Romulus Augustulus, a boy of 12 years old when he became emperor. It was his father Orestes who put him in the position to be a puppet emperor. Augustulus was appointed in 475, and his short reign ended in 476 when Odoacer, a German warlord, killed Augustulus' father. Odoacer made his way to Milan where the puppet emperor lived. Augustulus was offered retirement and a pension as he was sent away.

As a result of losing their emperor, the Roman Senate decided not to seek another, instead writing to their eastern counterpart:

> The majesty of a sole monarch is sufficient to pervade and protect, at the same time, both East and West. The west no longer required an emperor of its own; one monarch sufficed for the world.

Although 476 CE has become the designated end to the Western Roman Empire, it had been in steady decline for much longer. The deposition of the emperor simply acted as a suitable marker to end this particular chapter of European history.

All Was Not Lost

By the 5th century, the Roman Empire had extended far beyond Western Europe. It reached east along what is now the western Middle East and into Africa. Rome had not been at the center of the empire for several centuries. While the Romans certainly considered themselves the hub of their empire, there were many other places in the former empire that were largely unaffected by the fall of the city. As acknowledged by the Western Roman Senate, there was another part of the empire that remained fully functional and far more capable than Rome had been by the end of its reign.

The Roman Empire had two capitals at the time Rome was attacked. The second capital was to the east, and it was called Nicomedia. During the last centuries of the Roman Empire, there would be Roman emperors who lived in Nicomedia that would never visit Rome, and the words of the Roman Senate would be ignored in Nicomedia. In this part of the empire, the people in power focused on keeping a strong military. The city of Rome seemed to have conquered all of their potential rivals, so they settled into a tentative complacency. The Germanic tribes on their northern border never stopped being a problem, but the leaders seemed to have felt that the tribes were not a significant threat.

However, the eastern part of the Roman Empire had enemies on several sides. Retaining a much stronger military power was essential to repel attacks from their eastern and southern borders.

When Rome fell to the Goths, the entire eastern portion of the empire remained intact and was able to continue living as they had been living. They would become the protectors of European history (particularly the information about the Roman Empire which it had been a part of) and would become the new stewards of progress while Western Europe divided into what would become new countries with different power structures.

Chapter 2 – Stewards of the Future – The Rise of the Byzantine Empire

The fall of Rome is often thought of as the end of a golden era, a time when civilization thrived and philosophers pondered human nature. Once Rome was no longer the seat of power in Europe, all of the continent was suddenly plunged into a dark time when superstition reigned and the people were ignorant of even the most basic scientific ideas.

There are many obvious problems with this misrepresentation of the time following the fall of Rome and the beginning of the Middle Ages. The period between the 5th century and 13th century was not nearly so unenlightened or barbaric as people believe, and it certainly was not the Dark Ages that it has come to be called. Over much of the continent, the fall of Rome did little to change the daily lives of the general population. The people most affected by the fall were those who lived near Rome or those who had power throughout the empire.

All of the knowledge and brilliance from the height of the empire did not simply disappear, nor did the people suddenly become less mentally capable. Instead, many Romans left Rome, some looking for a simpler way of life, some for power they could not have obtained in Rome, and still others looking to rebuild their lives. However, those who were still proud to be Roman fled to the other capital of the empire—the city that would become the new capital of Europe, Constantinople.

The Founding of the Future Rome

The one thing to remember about the Byzantine Empire is that the people did not consider themselves to be any different than the Romans, except for where they lived. The region was not a completely separate empire that formed from the ashes of the Roman Empire; it was a part of the empire. It was more of a transition from Rome as the center of the empire to Constantinople as the center and with a transition to Greek instead of Latin as the primary language.

Constantinople was founded while Rome was still the center of civilized Europe. Constantine was the Roman emperor who ruled all of the Roman Empire, both the west and the east, from 306 to 337 CE. During his reign, he moved the empire's capital to Byzantium (the name of the city while he was emperor) in May of 330 CE. Initially, Constantine called the capital New Rome, but the name that stuck was the City of Constantine. Over time, the official name of the city would become Constantinople.

One of the attractions of this city was the natural defenses that surrounded it and the easy access to the harbor. Located between Europe and Asia, Constantinople was able to receive goods and news much faster than Rome, and it attracted a large number of people who wanted to live in a place that was more lively and thriving than Rome. To the astute observer, Rome had become stagnant. In contrast, Constantinople was growing and changing in ways that offered opportunities that many could not find in Rome.

When Constantine died, no one was able to keep the large empire under control. The solution that followed was to divide the empire into two halves and to have two different emperors control it together. Emperor Valentinian I divided the empire soon after he took power because he realized that he could not manage to sustain the empire as Constantine had. He took control over the west and his brother, Valens, ruled over the east. The next 200 years would show just how different the two regions were. As Rome decayed and fell, Constantinople established itself as the dominant force, the beacon of hope for the intellectuals, artists, merchants, and opportunists. They maintained a strong military, and rulers focused on the betterment of the empire.

The real power of the eastern empire began to show in 527 CE under Emperor Justinian. Under his control, the Byzantine Empire developed a military that would push east and west. As the western part of the empire stumbled and fell, the Byzantine Empire marched west, returning many of the cities and areas back to the fold. During its height, the Byzantine Empire would include much of what was once the Roman Empire. They would provide structure and assistance to these outer regions even as they pushed east and south, conquering areas that went well beyond Rome's reach.

Progress

The starting point for most of the men of the Renaissance was not the original teachings of the Romans but the teachings of the people who had fled Constantinople after it fell to the Ottoman Empire.

While Western Europe seemed to be evaluating itself, the Byzantine Empire built on the ideas and thoughts of the Romans. Some of the most magnificent buildings in European history were built in Constantinople, with the former Greek Orthodox cathedral of Hagia Sophia being perhaps the most impressive and well-known example. It still stands today, over 1,500 years after its construction.

Another major distinction between Western Europe and the Byzantine Empire was in their power and social structures. The power-hungry authorities of Europe began to claim their own lands, establishing feudal systems that put the majority of the people at the bottom with little room for advancement. The Byzantine Empire was far less oppressive of its people, offering opportunities to those with ideas and skills in its early years. Like many other empires before and since, its strength was in tapping the potential of many individuals regardless of social class. Talent and intellect were valued and listened to, just as they had been during the golden years of the Roman Empire. This created the thriving melting pot that would keep the culture and ideas of Rome going long after Western Europe had moved into a pettier, more mentally limited social structure. Over the centuries, the Byzantine Empire would suffer the same fate as Rome, with families and groups gaining power and influence and using it for selfish reasons instead of improving the empire. As the empire became more socially rigid, it would begin to stagnate and eventually fall.

Leaders Who Sustained and Surpassed Rome

There were many emperors and several empresses of the Byzantine Empire, some who were remarkable, many who were forgettable, and some who were as bad as Nero and Caligula. Over a millennium, there were several who stood out as pushing the empire forward or in delaying the inevitable decline.

Emperor Justinian and Empress Theodora are perhaps the most famous of the Byzantine rulers. Both Justinian and his wife were born into lower stations. He was born to peasants in 482 CE. The early history of Empress Theodora is less clear, but it is known that she worked as a courtesan for several years. Justinian became smitten with her because she was both clever and practical, and they married in 525. He became co-ruler with Emperor Justin I in 527. Justin died not long after, and Justinian became emperor. When two factions began to war in Constantinople, Theodora was the one who pressed Justinian to stay and fight to remove the factions that were destroying the city (instead of sitting back in safety as others had told him to do). Justinian successfully removed the threat, holding the empire together with his wife. Today's legal system is based on the *Codex Justinianus*, which was the code of law founded and implemented under Justinian. His wife worked alongside him, and many laws were named after her and her efforts. The Roman Catholic Church would even adopt many of the Byzantine laws during the Middle Ages, helping to provide a more progressive legal structure. Justinian was a great patron of the arts, and it was under his direction that the Hagia Sophia was built. Following Theodora's death, he had her interred in one of the places that they had helped to build together, the Church of the Holy Apostle. They held different religious beliefs, but they proved that these differences could be used as a strength as they successfully ruled over much of what was once the Roman Empire. After her death, Justinian did not accomplish any further major changes or improvements.

Emperor Heraclius ruled from 610 to 641 CE. During his reign, he managed to establish the direction and norms for his empire, making Greek the official language and creating a military that could expand the empire in almost all directions. Not all of his military campaigns were successful, and he lost some territories, including Mesopotamia and Egypt, to the growing Muslim population. Despite his losses, Heraclius is attributed with having a firm hand and minimizing or removing corruption so that his empire did not suffer the same fate as the Western Roman Empire.

Leo VI has a legacy that is more akin to that of Julius Caesar. When Leo VI became emperor in 886, he began to take power away from the Senate, which had retained the majority of the control of the government in the years prior to him taking the throne. Leo VI was unlike many of his predecessors as his earlier years had been focused primarily on scholarly pursuits and learning instead of the military. This gave him a distinct advantage since he was able to peacefully wrest control from those who had it, placing himself and future emperors in a much greater position of power. Over time, this situation would be just like the Roman Empire in that authority was with one person, and this would prove to be a part of the empire's undoing as no one person can properly manage an entire empire. This was very obvious as Leo VI suffered numerous military losses, some of them very costly, such as the war with the Bulgars who required an annual stipend after his loss to them. However, his reign saw more recordings of the history of the empire (not always objectively written), as well as adaptations of rules and laws to better fit the changing landscape. In a bid to ensure that the power he had amassed would pass on to his descendants, he married three different times in an effort to produce an heir. The third marriage was considered illegal, and the Byzantine Church was emphatic that he would not be allowed a fourth marriage when the third wife failed to produce an heir. As Henry VIII would do several hundred years later, Leo VI ignored the warnings of the Church and had an illegitimate son with a mistress. He then went on to have their union recognized, and his son eventually became the future emperor. No previous emperor would have been so successful in forcing the Church to ensure his legacy because no previous ruler had ever focused so much on taking control. It set up a dangerous precedent that would mean some people would later become rulers who were wildly unfit for the role instead of the emperor being the person best suited for the position.

Seeds of the Renaissance from the Byzantine Empire

Constantine was not a particularly religious man, but he understood that it was important to gauge the perceptions of his people. During his reign, it had become clear that Christianity had become a force that held far more sway than the old gods of the early Roman Empire. He realized that the best way to unite people was to convert the entire empire to Christianity.

For roughly the next millennium, most of Europe and the Byzantine Empire (which stretched through the Middle East and into Northern Africa at its peak) were Christian. In the beginning, the powers of the Church were shared over several major cities all across Europe and the empire. The rise of Rome as the seat of power for Christians showed how divided east and west were by the difference in their religion and ideology. The Great Schism is detailed in a later chapter, but it is important to understand that no part of the Byzantine Empire saw Rome as the religious center that all of Western Europe so revered during the Middle Ages. The Roman Catholic Church would emerge and claim to know the will of the Christian god. This would be the start of a power struggle that would last until the final years of the Byzantine Empire. Once the empire fell, the Church would become a much darker power that would ruthlessly remove anyone who disagreed with it. Some of the ruthlessness of the Catholic Church would emerge during the Middle Ages, but many of its most infamous acts would occur during the early modern era, such as the Inquisition and witch hunts.

As much credit as the Renaissance may get for bringing Europe out of the "Dark Ages," most of their work owed everything to the people of the Byzantine Empire, to those people of what was once the eastern part of the Roman Empire who never went through a dark period. While the Catholic Church was consolidating power in the west, the Byzantine Empire was encouraging free thought and would see the advancement of those ideas and concepts that the Renaissance would come to revere. Writing, theories, theology, and boundaries continued to be tested and furthered for 1,000 years. When Constantinople fell, some of the survivors returned to Rome and helped to trigger the Renaissance.

Chapter 3 – Reclaiming Spain and Expanding One of the Strongest and Earliest Kingdoms of the Middle Ages

There were two major powers that emerged by the end of the Middle Ages: Italy and Spain. While Italy was the seat of the former Roman Empire, Spain had always been on the periphery. There was nothing to indicate just how powerful the peninsula would one day become (Spain and Portugal would become prominent countries by the early modern era), particularly at the beginning of the Middle Ages. The men who sacked Rome eventually took up residence in the area that would one day become Spain, but with lands under their own control, they did not have any reason to keep the same structured military that had finally taken down Rome.

Another powerful force was growing and spreading across Africa during this time. They not only tested the strength of the new leaders of Europe, but they also threatened to expand far into Europe. This threat was stopped and forced to leave Spain by the military prowess and brilliant strategies of Charles Martel.

An Unfortunate Beginning

Charles Martel (also known as Karl Martell [German name] or Carolus Martellus [a Latin name]) was born to Pepin II of Herstal and a mistress. Pepin II was the Mayor of the Palace in Austrasia. Kings had no significant power at the time and primarily were leaders only in name. Mayors across the Frankish region were the ones who ruled over their regions. Pepin's only male heir was assassinated in 714, and Pepin did not long outlive him.

Since Charles was an illegitimate son, he was not even mentioned in the line of succession. This did not stop Charles from trying to take control of the region, even though he had three nephews who were closer in line to their grandfather (they were also too young to hold any position). Charles' claiming of the position of mayor of the palace soon caused problems, and rebellions began across the kingdom. By 719, though, he had managed to put down the rebellions.

Having successfully taken control of his father's realm, Charles set out to take control of the rest of the Frankish lands. One of his first attacks was against Odo the Great, the Duke of Aquitaine in France. At this time, he was unsuccessful. However, his efforts were successful elsewhere, and he defeated the Germanic tribes to the east. Charles helped to secure his position by supporting missionaries who were willing to go to the Germanic tribes and try to convert them to Christianity.

Charles Martel

As the Roman Empire disintegrated in Western Europe, the Muslim world experienced a rapid expansion. The Muslim Caliphs originated in modern-day Saudi Arabia, and the realms of the Muslims grew in every direction. They had a steady line of military successes that took them across Northern Africa. Having successfully defeated the Byzantine Empire in the Battle of

Yarmouk, the Strait of Gibraltar posed little problem to their continued expansion into the less well-defended Western Europe.

Although they were Muslim, they followed the Roman method of expansion. The areas that they conquered were allowed to keep their culture and religion; the defeated peoples just had to recognize the Caliph as the authority of the regions the Muslims conquered. This made it more palatable for people to surrender because life would largely go on as it had.

The biggest problem with this expansion was that the victorious Muslims pillaged and looted any temples, churches, or synagogues that they encountered. It was considered part of the spoils of their conquest.

Not only did Western Europeans find this distasteful (the Vikings had already followed this same method of conquering, and the forming European nations did not want to experience that again), they were also mortified by the idea of being conquered by Muslims. Many of the places that the Muslims occupied eventually converted to Islam. When they reached the border of France at the beginning of the 8th century, many of the nearby Goths took notice.

Before the Muslim forces arrived, Spain was largely controlled by the Visigoths, many of whom were direct descendants of the men who had sacked Rome a few centuries earlier. After a few hundred years, the Visigoths were not the same force that they had been, and they easily fell to the Muslim army.

The first real challenge the Muslims encountered was in Aquitaine. The leader of the opposing forces, Odo, was able to defeat the invaders, causing them to pause for the first time since they began to expand west. The Battle of Toulouse in 721 was the first time that Western Europe realized that they were not as safe as they had thought they were, but they had also proved that they could face the invaders. For the next 10 years, the Muslims continued to raid parts of southern France, but they did not push forward.

With the invaders chipping away at Odo's territory, Odo turned to Charles Martel, a Frankish king, for help. Charles agreed to assist as long as Odo agreed to recognize the Franks as the new authority in the region. Faced with being ruled by the Christian Franks or by the Muslims, Odo chose to be ruled by Christians. Charles continued to increase the strength and numbers in his army without the Muslims realizing the growing danger to the north.

The two forces met in 732 in Tours. Charles Martel soon demonstrated how he got his name (Martel translates to "The Hammer"). The first week of the encounter saw numerous skirmishes that were mostly a test to see how strong the other side was. The commander of the Muslims was Abdul Rahman Al Ghafiqi, and he had no idea just how large the opposing force was, nor did he learn about the size of Martel's army during the skirmishes. He did learn enough to request reinforcements, but Charles was also able to determine that more men would be needed, so he requested some of his most experienced and hardened soldiers to join him.

Up to that point, the Muslims had followed a predictable approach to their first attack. Instead of directly attacking, they sent in light cavalry and then heavy cavalry, wearing down their opponent. Given how successful the maneuver had been up until that point, there was no reason to believe that it wouldn't work again.

Unfortunately for the Muslims, Charles adopted a formation that had been employed by the ancient Greeks, using the foliage and terrain to protect the men from the cavalry. When Ghafiqi encountered Charles and his men, it came as a complete shock just how large their forces were. The Franks were able to withstand many of the cavalry's assaults because of their tight formation. When the Muslim cavalry finally did manage to break through the formation, Charles and his closest guards charged in to meet them.

While Charles was fighting on the front, some of his scouts were sent into the Muslim camps to act as a distraction. It worked. Some of the Muslim soldiers feared that the spoils they had accumulated over the last decade would be taken, so they tried to return to the camp to stop the scouts from looting. Their retreat from the field appeared to others in the army to be a full retreat. Confusion ensued, and Ghafiqi tried to correct it. He was killed, and the Franks quickly followed the retreating Muslim forces.

From the initial skirmishes to the end of the battle, only about a week had passed. The Muslims who survived the fighting took what they could carry and fled south. Charles was extremely cautious about following them though. In most battles, those retreating usually died, but Charles' men were on foot, making it easier for a larger number of the Muslim cavalry to survive the retreat. This made it difficult for Charles to determine how successful he was, so he sent scouts out to determine if an ambush awaited him and his men. After he realized that the Muslim force had in fact fled, he planned for the future.

In the Battle of Tours, it is thought that he lost about 1,000 men. In contrast, it was estimated that the Muslims lost between 8,000 and 10,000 men. Without their own commander, the Muslims realized that they had extended their forces too thin, and over time, they left Spain.

Both Charles and Odo became the heroes of Christian Europe. They managed to defeat one of the most brilliant Muslim commanders and drive the Muslims out of Western Europe. This was a feat that even the Byzantine Empire had not managed to do. Charles continued his campaigns in other parts of Europe in an effort to expand Frankish lands.

He retired from the military life he had known around 741 when he became ill. Preparing for his own demise, he left the rule of the lands he had taken to his sons Pepin the Short and Carloman. One of his descendants would acquire his military prowess and gained a name that is still known by most of the Western world today—Charlemagne.

Chapter 4 – Charlemagne – A Brief Return to the Empire

While Eastern Europe continued to thrive and grow, Western Europe was in a state of nearly complete disarray. People were fighting for scraps of the empire, seeking to create their own little power structures. The Middle Ages would be a time when nations would rise out of the ashes of the Roman Empire, but there was a time, under Charlemagne, when it appeared that Western Europe would return to a similar structure that it had seen under the Western Roman Empire.

A brilliant military strategist and inspirational leader, Charlemagne would accomplish what no one else had done since the fall of Rome—he would unite much of Western Europe under a single banner.

A Continent Divided

Once Rome lost control over the western part of Europe, many people saw it as an opportunity to become powerful, something they could not have done under a united Rome. However, not all of the people who took control were looking for power. The Germanic tribes that had caused so many problems for the Romans began to reclaim their lands or to fully control the lands that had been granted to them by the Romans. Since many of the Germanic tribes had not fully integrated into the Roman Empire, it was easy for them to return to their previous cultures and ways of life.

As territories fell under the control of many different groups, factions, and families, the infrastructure that Rome had built across Europe began to decay and fail. Roads became less safe to travel, both because of bandits and because the roads were no longer maintained. The water structures that had brought water to irrigate fields fell into disrepair, making some areas unworkable for farmers. As survival became less certain, many of the artistic endeavors and scientific pursuits were neglected. It is because of this decay and collapse of critical structures that people would one day point to the Middle Ages and call them the Dark Ages. Much of what the Romans and Western Europeans had taken for granted became rare as people focused on trying to make it through to the next day.

A term that has been more aptly applied to this time is the Migration period. People were free to move anywhere they wanted to without requiring permission from an authority. There was no single power structure defining the continent, although the Byzantine Empire would stretch into Western Europe during its height. Even then, they took more of a hands-off approach because they considered the people in the west to be more barbaric. The eastern empire shared ideas and helped but left many of the people in the west to do as they pleased.

The only exception during this time was under the Carolingian dynasty. That was established by one of the most famous European leaders during the Middle Ages—Charlemagne.

Born a King

Charlemagne was not born into obscurity. As the son of King Pepin the Short, Charlemagne was destined to take over the throne if he survived his early years. Pepin was the King of the Franks and lived in what is now Belgium. Born the eldest of Pepin's two sons in 742, Charlemagne was always going to rule his people. Pepin died in 768

CE, leaving his kingdom to be ruled by both of his sons, which seemed to keep the peace. However, Charlemagne's brother died unexpectedly in 771, leaving Charlemagne to manage their people and kingdom.

One of Charlemagne's strengths had always resided in his military abilities, and he soon launched military campaigns against neighboring kingdoms to strengthen and later expand his own kingdom. One of his most famous expansions occurred during the Saxon Wars. The Saxons were considered barbaric and cruel to Christian Europeans because they did not worship the Christian god. They seemed willing to commit all kinds of atrocities, although it is not certain how much of this assertion is true and how much of it was colored by the conquerors who would finally force the Saxons to submit. The Saxons were a very strong Germanic tribe that posed a threat to Charlemagne; at least, he perceived them as a threat to him and his kingdom. These campaigns began in 772 and would last until Charlemagne finally forced them to not only surrender but to also become Christians. His desire to conquer others did not stop with the Saxons though. Pushing south, he took control over the northern part of what is modern-day Italy. In 778, he marched into the northern part of Spain and drove out the Moors. By 800, he had taken control over much of Europe.

Becoming Emperor

During 800 CE, a rebellion erupted in Rome. The role of pope was given to a man who was considered the most deserving, Leo III. When Paschal, a blood relative to the recently deceased Pope Adrian I, was not selected for the position, he was angry. Working with conspirators, he planned to maim Pope Leo III, making him unfit for office.

As Pope Leo moved through a procession of chanting Christians, the conspirators attacked him. Some drove away the other participants in the procession while others attacked the pope directly. They attempted to both blind and silence him by stabbing his eyes then trying to remove his tongue. Pope Leo III was critically injured, but the wounds did not kill him, even after the group dragged him to the closest chapel and attacked him a second time.

Pope Leo III and some of his loyal followers managed to flee from Rome and cross the Alps. Charlemagne considered himself a devout Christian, so when they reached Charlemagne's lands, he readily accepted the pope and offered him protection. When he was ready, the pope was taken back to Rome under Charlemagne's security.

What followed was some tense back and forth between the conspirators and the pope. The conspirators accused the pope of whatever they could think of, and Leo wanted to see the attackers tried. Charlemagne finally stepped in and ordered the execution of the conspirators. However, the pope was not willing to see them killed, and pointing to the pacifism of Christ and the directive to forgive, he asked that the conspirators be spared. Instead of death, they were exiled.

To repay Charlemagne's kindness and help, Leo crowned him the Emperor of Rome, establishing a very dangerous norm that would cause problems in Western Europe for centuries. Although Leo may have only meant to repay Charlemagne, the pope who came after him would point to his declaration to show that the Church had power over rulers. This precedent would be tested many times over the centuries and would finally lead to some of the most violent wars and acts of violence in European history as nations would take sides with or against the Church.

For Charlemagne, the declaration did not change much. It simply gave him a stronger claim to help protect Italy and Rome. He also would work with the pope, maintaining a strong relationship until his death. As Charlemagne increased his kingdom, he gave Leo some of the spoils, and this was used to help create magnificent edifices and buildings, taking the pope further and further from the religion he had espoused when he was chosen to lead the Church.

Following Charlemagne's death, the pope's life would again be threatened by conspirators. As if to demonstrate just how much Leo enjoyed the power he had because of Charlemagne, once he found out about the plot, he had the conspirators arrested and executed for the crime.

The Byzantine Empire was angered by the actions of Leo as well. They considered the lands theirs, and the pope was one of several religious figureheads of the Christian Church. He had acted without their consent and established a second emperor. However, the empire did not do anything notable to correct the problem, so very little came of Leo's actions. Charlemagne was crowned on December 25, 800 CE, but he would not live 15 years afterward. Without Charlemagne, the kingdom he had created crumbled.

Chapter 5 – Otto I and His New Empire

Although he is less well known today than Charlemagne, Otto I was a Saxon king who expanded his kingdom well beyond what anyone else who came after him would achieve. Perhaps even more impressive, Otto I spent a considerable amount of time fighting his own family for control over the kingdom and later his empire. His rule as the King of Germany would last from 936 until 973, and it would be a period of unrest and bloodshed.

Unlike Charlemagne, much of what Otto I did to help Rome was done as much to help himself. He did not appear to be a particularly spiritual man, and much of his time and attention went to increasing his military strength and dominating those who were beneath him. The lands he would bring into his empire would be the foundation for what would later become the Holy Roman Empire, which would last well into the early modern era. By the time of his death, Otto controlled most of the same lands that Charlemagne had held.

An Uncertain Heir

Being born to a duke of the Saxons that eventually became king did not guarantee that Otto would become king. He was not the only son of the king, and it was up to the Saxons to determine who would follow King Henry the Fowler. It is known that he was the son of the king's second wife and that he was born in 912. Very little else is known of Otto's early life because there are no records. Given his military brilliance, some historians believe that he was probably engaged in some of the military campaigns that King Henry led against the surrounding Germanic tribes.

Otto married the daughter of an English noble in 930, and she had a daughter and a son with him. King Henry had appointed Otto to be his successor, and following the king's death in 936, the Saxons agreed with the late king's choice with Otto being elected to take his father's place that same year. The crowning ceremony was held in Cologne at Aachen, a place that is said to have been Charlemagne's favorite spot to reside during his reign.

However, the early part of Otto's reign was marked with feuding and fighting as the great duchies around him sought to take his power; it also didn't help that members of his own family resented the fact that Otto was chosen to be his father's successor.

Taking Control

King Henry's choice would prove to be the correct one since Otto would take down all of those who opposed him. While his father had never been able to exert complete control over the dukes within his domain, Otto managed to consolidate his power, removing most of the authority that the dukes had. This was part of the reason for much of the strife in the early years as he exerted his newfound powers.

The first major test of the new king came in 937, the year after Otto was crowned. Thankmar was Otto's half-brother, and he worked with a faction of dukes from his own realm to attack Otto. Thankmar died during the battle, and one of the dukes was deposed following the fighting. The other duke submitted to Otto but would join with another duke and one of the king's other brothers, Henry, just two years later.

Henry was the king's younger brother, and some of the dukes supported his revolt against Otto in 939. Because of his heritage, Henry was able to get the backing of Louis IV, the King of France, to lead a revolt against Otto. The dukes who fought with Henry died, including the duke who had joined in the first rebellion. Otto did not punish his own brother as he did to some of the others involved, forgiving Henry instead of executing or exiling him.

Still believing that he was a better choice as king, Henry banded together with conspirators in a bid to assassinate his brother just two years later. When Otto learned of the plot in 941, he had all of the people who joined in his brother's conspiracy killed, but he again forgave Henry. This second forgiveness seemed to have finally persuaded Henry that Otto was the superior leader, and he became a faithful supporter of his brother for the rest of his life. In turn, Otto would make Henry the Duke of Bavaria. The other dukedoms were divided between other members of Otto's family.

Even while he was fighting with his own family and people, Otto managed to expand his kingdom. He was able to defeat the Slavs to the east of his kingdom and took control over some of Denmark. In 950, he was able to finally defeat Prince Boleslav I of Bohemia, with Otto requiring a tribute from the prince. France was the biggest problem because it continued to attack Otto from the west, but he was able to rebuff their claims on Lotharingia.

One of the most intriguing conquests of Otto I was in northern Italy. Following the death of her husband, King Lothair II's widow, Adelaide, was left with little support in Italy. She was captured and held as a prisoner by King Berengar II in 951. Her plea for help reached Otto. His own wife had died six years before, so he found what appeared to be the best solution to Adelaide's plight: He took his army into Italy and married her, resulting in the addition of the title of King of Italy to his name.

While Otto was expanding his kingdom, his only son by his first wife, Liudolf, began to act to obtain his own power. Joining with several other prominent Germanic figures, Liudolf started a revolt against his father. It was the first time a family member had posed a real threat to Otto, and he initially had to withdraw his military and support to Saxony. Luck was on Otto's side though as the Magyars (likely descendants from Attila's hordes who lived at the same time as the more famous Huns and Turks) invaded the region where Liudolf and his supporters resided in 954. With his military stretched thin, Liudolf submitted to Otto in 955. With the revolt out of the way, Otto was able to easily sweep into the area and deal with the Magyars. The Battle of Lechfeld was a decisive battle that left the Magyars so crushed that they would never again seek to invade Germany.

Beginning of an Empire

Otto had proved adept both in military and political prowess, expanding his domain while many other smaller rulers bickered and squabbled over their territories. By 961, he was thinking about his successor, and he chose his son Otto, whom he had with Adelaide. Otto was only six, so King Otto wanted to ensure that this son would be his successor. He held an election that resulted in his young son being elected to the position, and the young Otto was crowed that same year as the joint-ruler of Germany.

With the question of succession out of the way, King Otto returned to Italy. King Berengar II, who had taken Adelaide prisoner, was again causing problems, this time for Pope John XII. Otto lent his support to the pope, and in return, he was crowned Holy Roman Emperor in 962. The crowning was followed by an agreement, known as the Privilegium Ottonianum, that dictated the terms of the relationship between the emperor and pope. The amount of control future emperors would have may or may not have been influenced by the events of the following year. Pope John XII worked with Berengar in a conspiracy against Otto. After defeating Berengar, Otto had John removed from his position, claiming that his conduct had been unbecoming for the pope's religious position. Otto then chose the next pope, Leo VIII. This new pope died in 965, having served for only a very short period of time. Next, Otto selected John XIII, who was widely disliked by the people. They revolted against his choice, forcing Otto to return to Italy to put down the new rebellion.

With all of the trouble coming from Italy, Otto chose to remain there for several years to ensure that order was restored. He trekked into lands that belonged to the Byzantine Empire, but he was unsuccessful in taking control of the southern part of Italy. Emperor Otto also took the opportunity to ensure that his son Otto would become the next ruler and had him crowned as co-emperor. This position was further solidified in 972 when Emperor Otto negotiated for the hand of Theophano, (who was a princess in the Byzantine Empire) for his son.

Otto would finally return to his home where he died in 973.

While he is remembered for his military strength, Otto believed in education, and under his reign, the territories experienced a type of renaissance. Those he appointed into religious positions often developed supportive communities for culture, and some of the most beautiful buildings were begun as a result. It was a time when intellect and architecture were further advanced during the Middle Ages, proving that the time was not so dark or uncultured as people have often claimed.

Otto I is widely considered to be the first emperor of the Holy Roman Empire. After the empire of Charlemagne, Otto's empire was the largest across the continent and would remain so for centuries. While some consider Otto's empire to be a continuation of Charlemagne's, others credit Otto with starting the Holy Roman Empire. Otto's empire did cover largely the same lands, but he did have to unite them under him as there was no strong leader to take over after Charlemagne died. Between the reigns of the two great military leaders, the region had become divided by smaller rulers. Even after it was united, the Holy Roman Empire would be far less cohesive than countries like France, Italy, Spain, and England. This reflects just how large the area was and how many different cultures were within it.

Chapter 6 – The Great Schism

It would be easy to consider the Great Schism as an inevitable split between Eastern and Western Europe. From the time that the two different centers of the Roman Empire were established, it seemed as though it was only a matter of time for them to split and drift apart. When Rome fell and Constantinople remained largely unaffected by the loss, there seemed to be no returning to the time when they were all part of the same empire.

The difference between Western and Eastern Europe during the Middle Ages was like the difference between the Roman Empire and the untamed tribes that they fought against. Although the foundation was still the same for both sides, they grew apart. This ultimately resulted in a divide in the Christian world that has never been reconciled.

Two Different Worlds under One Religion

The way the Byzantine Empire and Western Europe regarded the Christian religion proved to be the breaking point that eventually divided the east and west. There were plenty of divisions before religion became a major issue. For instance, Greek was spoken in the Byzantine Empire, and although there was a wide range of languages across Western Europe, it still retained Latin as the core for many of the languages that developed. Most of Western Europe clung to Latin, using it even today as the foundation for scientific and legal terms.

The Byzantines retained much of the culture and intellect that the west so revered. They viewed the west as barbarians, which is not surprising considering the fact that the west was the entity that eventually sacked and destroyed Rome. Western Europe had many fiefdoms, and infighting seemed almost like a pastime to the peoples fighting for the scraps of the Roman Empire. By comparison, the Byzantine Empire not only retained the pride and culture of Rome, but they also often banded together as a whole, keeping invaders from penetrating the heart of the empire for centuries. Rarely did the west pose a serious threat to anything that the Byzantine Empire had.

When you think of the Dark Ages, the image is of Western Europe, and this is almost certainly similar to how the people of the Byzantine Empire viewed Western Europe at the time. It is very likely that their view of Western Europe during the Middle Ages contributed to the term the "Dark Ages." This term certainly never applied to the Byzantine Empire, but there are reasons why people consider it to be an accurate description for Western Europe. Many of the pursuits and structures that defined the Roman Empire were almost completely lost during the Middle Ages in the areas that had been under Western Roman control. Their technology rotted, and science came almost to a grinding halt.

Occasionally, a man emerged and temporarily united parts of Western Europe. It became clear that the pope in Rome felt that he spoke for all of the Christian world when he crowned a new emperor. The first example was when Charlemagne was crowned as emperor, but that was not the only instance (Otto I would be the first in a line of successive emperors of the region). This was considered as a serious affront to the people of the Byzantine Empire as it seemed to exclude not only their rulers but also their power over the Christian religion. The people in the Byzantine Empire, who followed the Eastern Orthodox Church, considered the Patriarch of Constantinople to be the highest authority in the Christian world, while naturally, the west, who followed the Catholic Church, thought that the pope in Rome was.

Two Different Interpretations of the Christian Teachings

The ideological differences between the two Churches were numerous, and over the centuries, tensions festered. The first major break between the east and west was linked to iconoclasm. According to the Byzantine Emperor Leo III, any replication of religious figures was considered an idol. He put forward this belief around 726 and then tried to force the Roman pope to conform to the declaration. When Rome remained steadfastly in favor of keeping the art depicting religious figures, Leo III sent his military to enforce his declaration that it was heretical. When military force failed, Leo III confiscated lands that belonged to the pope and placed them under the control of Constantinople.

Up until this time, the pope in Rome had been nominated and selected by the Byzantine Emperor. After this incident, the church in Rome started to elect its own pope without any confirmation or input from Constantinople.

Many of the people in the Byzantine Empire also supported the use of art as a way to depict events and people that were key to the history of their religion. They pointed out that people who were illiterate had no other way of understanding the teachings on their own, arguing that it was vital to continue with the works of art. The internal strife in the Byzantine Empire was finally resolved in 843 (called the Triumph of Orthodoxy), but it was too late to atone for the actions of Leo III more than 100 years earlier.

Another point of contention between the two teachings was on whether to use leavened or unleavened bread as part of communion.

To the Romans, communion was linked to Christ's Last Supper, and they opted to use unleavened bread as he had. To the Byzantine people, communion was about celebrating Christ's rising from the dead, so they used leavened bread.

However, the most significant difference in ideologies was about the nature of Jesus Christ himself. The Roman pope and those close to him believed that Christ was holy, and they elevated him to be equal to their god. They believed in this so strongly that they added it to the Nicene Creed, a statement of belief used in Christian liturgy, in a piece called the filioque. This was added by Pope Sergius IV at the beginning of the 11th century. The people of the Byzantine Empire disagreed. They not only refused to add it to the Nicene Creed, but they had Pope Sergius and all Roman popes after him removed from their official list of leaders that were part of the Christian world. Roughly 50 years later, the Roman Catholic Church called the Eastern Church heretical because they did not include the filioque passage in the Nicene Creed.

In addition to these diverging ideas on religion, the thought processes followed by both groups of people also differed significantly. The west tended to follow the Roman love for laws and firm lines that explained all aspects of religion (which proved to be not only problematic later, but also antithetical to science). By contrast, the Eastern Church did not think that humans would ever fully understand the mysteries and decisions of their god, so they accepted that humans would never understand everything. They also believed that people needed to have a relationship with their god, instead of the western approach that felt that the people required mediation through their version of the church.

The Christian World Divided

In the past, tensions occasionally flared, but both the eastern and western parts of the Christian world allowed people to follow whichever version of the religion they preferred. The teachings of the eastern beliefs were practiced in Western Europe, including in Italy, and western beliefs were taught in the east, even in Constantinople.

The begrudging tolerance to each other's ideas faltered when the Western Church began to consolidate power through reforms. Some of the changes were positive, as they sought to rein in many of the abuses that were perpetrated by clerics who sought personal gain and enrichment. The reforms also meant putting more power in the hands of the pope.

In 1053, Pope Leo IX tried to not only claim to be the head of all of the Western Church but tried to claim control over all the Christian world. He had all of the churches in southern Italy that followed the eastern practices and ideologies to either conform to the practices of the west or be shut down. In response, Michael I Cerularius, the Patriarch of Constantinople, had all of the western churches closed in the capital.

Leo IX sent a representative to the Byzantine capital in 1054 to try to force Patriarch Michael I Cerularius to accept the Roman pope as the head of the Christian Church. Two months passed as the two sides waited for a response. During a service being held in the Hagia Sophia (the Patriarch's cathedral in Constantinople), the pope's representative, Cardinal Humbert, marched up to the front of the cathedral and laid a bull (a religious decree) on the altar, stating that Michael and all of his followers had been excommunicated. This action was not pressed by the pope but by Cardinal Humbert who did not like the Byzantines. It actually could not have come from the pope because Pope Leo IX died not long after the cardinal left Rome. Humbert and the other representatives left Constantinople two days after his interruption of the service to excommunicate the eastern head of the Christian Church. Michael soon excommunicated the pope (not knowing that Leo IX was already dead) and everyone who played a role in the excommunication perpetrated in Hagia Sophia.

It was not the first time that leaders on both sides excommunicated the other, but it had always been reconciled before any long-term damage was done. This excommunication could have been amended soon after the problem arose too. With Pope Leo IX dead, Victor II was elected to the position. He could have revoked the actions on that day, but that was not the path he chose to take.

A couple of attempts at reconciliation were attempted over the next 150 years, and the relationship between the two churches was friendly, even if it was strained. However, any hope at reconciliation was completely destroyed by the western participants in the Fourth Crusade who chose to attack Constantinople instead of their target in Jerusalem.

This also foreshadowed the dark direction that the Roman Catholic Church would take over the next few centuries. The popes became increasingly power hungry and vicious. They did not allow anyone to question their "divine" laws and had anyone who did killed for being a heretic. The Roman Catholic Church pushed Western Europe into a more backward mindset as they had scientists and anyone who did not agree with the Church's teaching on history and science tortured and/or killed. And the Inquisition, judicial institutions meant to combat heresy, sought to stamp out any questioning of the Church's authority.

As one can see, the Catholic Church became increasingly intolerant after the Great Schism. This is one of the main contributors to why people now consider the Middle Ages to be the Dark Ages. The backward thinking forced on people by the Catholic Church was not used in the Eastern Orthodox Church. There, science, thinking, and spirituality on an individual level were encouraged and welcomed by the Patriarch of Constantinople.

The World's Two Dominant Christian Religions

The Great Schism created two primary churches in the Christian world: Eastern Orthodox and Roman Catholic. Today, Catholics are the largest Christian denomination in the world, with an estimated 1.3 billion people subscribing to the religion. There are several sects that make up this estimate, including Eastern Rite Catholics (which includes Catholics of the Byzantine and Ukrainian Greek Churches). Roman Catholics have by far the largest population in the Catholic Church, however.

With an estimated 200-260 million followers, Eastern Orthodox is the second largest denomination. The majority of the members for this denomination are in Eastern Europe, such as Russia, the Balkans, and Romania.

The Great Schism is probably one of the reasons that people don't know as much about the Byzantine Empire. They were excluded for most (if not all) of the art and history told in the west, who did not recognize them as the continuation of the Roman Empire. The Byzantine Empire, however, was far more similar to the Roman Empire than the feuding west, and when the Byzantine Empire fell to the Ottoman Empire in 1453, those who fled had to conform to what they considered to be the more barbaric world of Western Europe. This does not negate what the Byzantine Empire contributed to knowledge and preserved from the Roman Empire, but it does relegate it to more of a footnote in early Western European history as their history was brought with the refugees.

Chapter 7 – The Famous (or Infamous) Crusades – 1095 to 1291

When people discuss the Middle Ages, there is one thing that repeatedly comes up in the conversation—the Crusades. They have been reimagined and discussed for centuries, which has made it difficult for the people of today to fully understand them. Many people have their own misconceptions, which often helps to perpetuate the hatred and bloodshed that should have ended long ago.

The Crusades pitted the three primary Western religions against each other. Christians and Muslims were the primary perpetrators of the horrors known as the Crusades, and the followers of Judaism were sometimes pulled into the battles as they had the same claim to the Holy Land as the other two religions. Christianity and Islam were actually strongly influenced by Judaism, and all three religions were far more similar to each other than they were different.

One of the reasons why the Crusades remain so prominent in the minds of the Western world is because they dominated so much of the politics across Europe for 200 years. Preparations for the first Crusade started in 1095, and the last Crusade ended in 1291. The number of Crusades that occurred is debatable.

The Holy Land

While the Romans still retained their power and control over their empire, the three religions recognized that they had far more in common with each other. They were all persecuted for their beliefs, and all three claimed that there was only one god while many of the other civilizations worshiped their own pantheons, including the Romans themselves. After the fall of Rome though, the three religions grew and sought to take control of the place where their respective religions either began or were significant to their history.

The Muslim world began to expand several centuries after the fall of Rome. Western Europe was shielded from the expansion by the Byzantine Empire to the east, and the people in control of the Byzantine Empire also sought to expand and keep the regions under their banner. However, during the 11th century, Muslims managed to take control of a large swathe of land, including many places that had once been under Roman and, later, Byzantine control, including the Holy Land. Christians had lost about two-thirds of their land, including parts of Spain (although the Muslims were stopped from making further inroads into the European continent by Charles Martel in the 8th century).

Christians were outraged that so many of the lands that were important to their religion, particularly Jerusalem, were now under the control of Muslims. There was a growing desire to reclaim the lands that they felt belonged to them because of their religion, and at the end of the 11th century, they decided that it was finally time to reclaim them.

This became a Christian belief, that certain lands belonged to them and must be protected, which lasted for about 200 years, with men going off to fight and die in foreign lands for a religion that, at its core, was pacifist in nature. Despite Jesus teaching his followers to turn the other check, the popes and rulers wanted bloodshed for perceived slights. It helped to show just how far removed the religion was from its original teachings, but few questioned it.

Each primary player had his own desires and plans for the land. The Byzantine emperors wanted to regain the lands that they had lost to Muslim invasions. The pope in Italy wanted to generate more power and have more people recognize him as the Christian spiritual leader. Knights felt obligated to fight for their faith following their moral code and the codes of chivalry (although they also sought wealth and spiritual gain in the next life—they weren't altruists). And merchants wanted to wrest control of the lucrative trade with the east from the Muslims.

Though the Crusades were framed as a religious necessity, they were anything but that. Knights tended to be the most well-meaning participants, and many leaders were attracted to the idea of being among the faithful to help "free" the Holy Land. Still, some of the leaders wanted to get something out of it. At least the merchants tended to be honest about their selfish causes.

The First Crusade

The First Crusade was several years in the making. It began when the Byzantine Empire lost control of Jerusalem in 1087. The empire was beyond its peak at this point, as was evident by their inability to repel the invaders, and their empire was considerably smaller than it had been during its height. Emperor Alexios I Komnenos wanted to take back Jerusalem, but he knew that he could not do it alone. With the Holy Land under the control of Muslims, he knew that removing the threat would be considered important to the Roman Catholic Church. The threat of Muslims was far greater than the threat of Eastern Orthodox Christianity, and the emperor knew that the Catholic pope had adequate personal incentive to help.

Pope Urban II had already helped the emperor (in 1091) to fend off nomads who were invading the empire near the Danube. This time, though, he stood to gain far more prestige as an instrument for removing the Muslim scourge from Christian lands. Of course, his goal was to consolidate and expand his power, but by vilifying the Muslims, Urban knew that he would be able to sell the idea better to the rest of the people of the Roman Catholic Church and its believers. One of the primary reasons why he felt compelled to accumulate more power was because of the influence that the Holy Roman Empire had maintained over the Church since Otto I had intervened to help Pope John XII. There had been times when Holy Roman Emperors forced the pope to leave Rome, and Pope Urban II wanted to prevent that from happening in the future. He wanted to stand above all other people in Europe, including the people in the Byzantine Empire. It was his hope that he would be able to reunite the recently split churches and become the head of a much larger church. By helping the emperor, he wanted to become the unquestioned ruler of everything in both Western and Eastern Europe.

Pope Urban II was a brilliant strategist. He knew that by casting the Muslims as villains, he would be able to paint the lives of Christians living under them as being in constant danger (similar to the kinds of danger Muslims and Jewish people in Christian lands faced, despite the fact that Muslims took an approach more similar to Rome, letting people keep their religion as long as they paid taxes). Urban also emphasized that the Holy Land belonged to the Christians and that their god would want them to reclaim it. By pointing out that the Muslims already posed a threat, having only recently been removed from Spain in 1085, he was able to make the case that it was a crisis that could not be ignored.

Urban II planned and carried out a call to arms in November of 1095 at the Council of Clermont in Aquitaine. The appeal was made to the knights, who often were seen as the most virtuous and the leaders of the hearts of the people. It was their duty to defend the Christian world and reclaim what was theirs by divine right. Should they choose to fight in the Crusade, all of their sins would be forgiven and their place in the next life would be assured. It was a pilgrimage unlike any other and with very high stakes.

Pilgrimages to the Holy Land were common; however, they were typically done as part of a penance. With religion being integral to the lives of most of the people of Europe, the idea that they could be forgiven for any sins they had committed (and possibly any they would commit) was very tempting. It was also the first time that the Church had openly condoned violence, this time in the name of a man who preached nonviolence and who would have rejected the idea. However, the pope wasn't doing it for his god; he was starting the Crusade for himself.

Word spread, largely by the pope's influence, that the Muslims were defiling Christian statues, monuments, and buildings. False accounts of Christians being tortured and killed were also spread (the fairly rare torturing of Christians by Muslims would pale in comparison to what the Inquisition would do to its own people during the early modern era though). All of this resulted in a large army of Christians answering the call to arms.

The knights were perhaps the most likely to gain on a personal level (such as the spoils of fighting and more recognition at home), but they also faced a heavy upfront cost in joining the Crusade. Many monasteries were willing to provide loans to knights so that they could be properly equipped. Many leaders across Europe also joined in the First Crusade, joining the knights in this perceived holy war. They also ordered some of their own knights to join, so it was not always a voluntary act by all participants.

Some of the people who answered the call were women and children (squires were often young, sometimes even still children). They would serve to help with the efforts by supporting the fighters instead of actually fighting. Peasants could also earn their freedom from a feudal lord by taking up arms and joining the Crusade. They could also become exempt from specific taxes and fees, have debt payments delayed, and could even reverse excommunication.

The propaganda was incredibly effective at drawing out supportive Christians, and it is estimated that 90,000 people left on the First Crusade in 1096. It was so popular that it would be dubbed "The People's Crusade." Those that reached Constantinople pledged themselves to Emperor Alexios, and he sent them south to reclaim the Holy Land.

Their path to Jerusalem was mixed with successes and failures. Just as the Christian world was not a single entity, the Muslim world was also divided and there was considerable infighting. This helped the Crusaders, and in 1099, they finally reached Jerusalem. By the end of the summer, they had slaughtered almost everyone who was not under the Western Christian god, including the massacre of Eastern Christians. They were perpetrating the very crimes that had rallied them to go south to the Holy Land in the first place. A ruler was elected to manage the city, and in 1100, Baldwin I became the Crusader king of Jerusalem. Pope Urban II never learned of the successful reclaiming of the city though because he died not long after it happened, and word did not travel quickly in the Middle Ages.

1099 is considered the end of the First Crusade, which had been marginally successful. Although they recaptured Jerusalem, it did not complete any of the personal goals sought by those in power and corrupted many of those who participated. Nor would they hold the land for long, turning the Holy Land into a killing field for about 200 years.

A 200-Year-Old Religious Tradition

The First Crusade was simply the start of an idea that would grip the minds of many men who wanted power, and the Crusades became increasingly corrupted as people sought personal gain instead of fighting because of supposed religious obligations. There would be seven or more sanctioned Crusades (there is some debate on how many were backed by the Church), and many crusades that were started without the Church's approval.

The number of religious wars carried out by the Christians became increasingly less effective as well. The Second Crusade was so disastrous that one of the leaders, King Louis VII of France, finally strained his marriage to Eleanor of Aquitaine to the breaking point. Their marriage was annulled, and she married the English king, Henry II, a few months after the divorce.

Their son, Richard I of England (often called Richard the Lionheart), managed to settle on a truce with Saladin when he participated in the Third Crusade (1189 to 1192), but on his return home, he was captured in Germany. He had fought alongside Philip II of France and the Holy Roman Emperor Frederick I during the Crusade, but that did not matter once it was over. His mother paid his ransom so that Richard I could return to wage further wars against France.

Christian Against Christian

By the beginning of the 13th century, the Crusades had all but lost any moral bearing. Perhaps the greatest damage done by the Crusades was to Constantinople. To the people of the Byzantine Empire, the idea of a religious war was entirely foreign, and they did not understand the Western zeal to kill in the name of Jesus. To the people of the empire, it was about reclaiming the region that they had once controlled. Having assistance was welcome, although the mistrust between Eastern and Western Christianity became increasingly transparent. They saw their Western counterparts as being barbaric and uncivilized, something that the Western Europeans would often reinforce with their mob-like behavior and looting of areas that they were meant to take.

The Fourth Crusade (1202 to 1204) began like the previous three, with the goal of retaking Jerusalem from the Muslims. It went awry before they had made any progress though. The Crusaders amassed in Venice, hoping to travel to Egypt to begin the fighting. The Venetians that they encountered demanded a price to transport them across the Mediterranean Sea that was too high for the Crusaders to pay. Seeing a unique opportunity, the Venetians said that if the Crusaders would reclaim Zara, Egypt (which had recently defected), they would take them to Egypt, and the Crusaders agreed.

Upon finding out what had happened, Pope Innocent III was infuriated that they had chosen to attack somewhere much closer to home, as well as at the Venetians for repurposing his holy war for their own financial gain. Not only did he excommunicate the Venetians, but he also excommunicated the Crusaders, many of whom wanted to be absolved of sins, not blocked from heaven in their afterlife (the pope did later rescind the excommunication of non-Venetians, however).

It is uncertain exactly what happened to instigate the next move by the Crusaders, but instead of seeking to reclaim Jerusalem, they attacked the capital of the Byzantine Empire, Constantinople. The Doge of Venice, Enrico Dandolo, had a contentious relationship with the capital after being expelled from it years earlier. As one of the leading Venetians, he certainly played a role in the terrible decision to use a Christian war against other Christians. Some of the Crusaders might have believed that the pope would view them more favorably if they were able to hand him control over all of the Christian world. Whatever the reason for this heinous act, the Fourth Crusade never really left Europe, completely warping any notion that it was religious or even sanctified anymore.

There is no doubt that the Crusaders were impressed by what they saw when they first glimpsed the city. Constantinople had become one of the brightest cities in the world, and the important buildings showed the wealth of the people. Whatever awe the Crusaders originally felt, it turned to greed very quickly.

Much like the Visigoths had managed to sack Rome, the Crusaders sacked Constantinople. They found it an easy target, and the Western

Christians committed all of the kinds of atrocities against other Christians that had originally spurred them to action against the Muslims for the first few Crusades. This included the theft of many priceless artifacts, some of which had been preserved since the Roman Empire.

The English historian J.J. Norwich best describes the attack and results: "By the sack of Constantinople, Western civilization suffered a loss greater than the burning of the library of Alexandria in the fourth century or the sack of Rome in the fifth—perhaps the most catastrophic single loss in all history."

While the Western Christians were perhaps too uneducated and selfish to understand the significance of the art and works, the Byzantines had a full understanding and were flabbergasted by the sheer barbarity of people who claimed to be members of the same religion. It confirmed their opinion that Western Europe was no more than a group of barbarians. However, by this point, the Byzantine Empire was waning, and there was little they could do about the situation.

The city would be divided by the Venetians and those who had allied themselves with the immoral men. The Byzantine Empire would not fully reform into an empire until 1261. It would never again be the empire that it had once been, and in 1453, it would finally disappear under the invasion of the Ottoman Turks.

The west would continue to crusade until the end of the 13th century (there were other Crusades afterward, but they were not sanctioned by the Church). However, the Crusades were largely ineffective, causing more strife back home as people began to resent paying taxes for wars in foreign lands. Eventually, leaders decided to keep the fighting closer to home and try to take the lands of neighboring countries instead of fighting in lands that they could not hope to keep under their control.

Chapter 8 – Forging a New England

The small islands off the coast of continental Europe have always held a particular fascination. England, in particular, has always done things differently than the people on the mainland, and this was no different during the Middle Ages. While men were fighting for large swathes of land in most of Europe, the people on the British Isles were struggling for control of a much smaller area. After the fall of Rome, the evolution of the power structure became the stuff of legend.

Even if they do not know exactly what they are, most of the Western world has heard of the Battle of Hastings and the Magna Carta. Both of these events occurred during the Middle Ages and helped to create the nation that would one day have an empire that reached nearly every continent across the globe.

The Battle of Hastings 1066

The Battle of Hastings put an end to the question of succession that had plagued England since the ascension of King Edward.

Edward was born during a turbulent time in English history. His father, King Æthelred II and his wife Emma of Normandy (the daughter of Richard I) had a legitimate claim to the throne.

However, the invasion by the Danes in 1013 CE caused them to flee. They took up residence in Normandy (part of modern-day northern France) where they lived in exile for a year. Edward accompanied several diplomats to England where they negotiated the return of Æthelred II as king. Unfortunately, the restored king died soon after in 1016. Seeing an opportunity, the Danes again returned and invaded the island. Edward returned to a life of exile for several decades.

In 1041, Edward finally returned to England to live in the court that had been established under his half-brother, King Harthacnut of Denmark (they shared the same mother). The king named his half-brother to be his heir. Harthacnut died the following year in 1042. Edward did not delay, quickly taking his place as king and taking all of the lands under his mother's control. Despite the fact that Edward was the rightful king, Emma (who had a long history of plotting against the kings with Godwin, Earl of Wessex) plotted against her son, in part because she wanted to retain control as queen. Despite Emma's failure to stop her son's ascension, her frequent co-conspirator Godwin retained considerable power and ruled in all but name for 11 years. Edward appeared to be content with the arrangement in the beginning, having spent much of his life far from London. Godwin had the support of the people, and Edward was aware that he was not as popular or commanding as the man who had lived in England through decades of unrest.

In 1045, Edward married Godwin's daughter to give the powerful man blood relations to the throne. However, the king and the shadow king did not always agree on issues and resolutions. In 1049, they had irreconcilable differences, and Edward began to take a larger role in the governing of the realm. Two years later, he would make the Godwin family outlaws, including his own wife. Unfortunately for the king, his reliance on and favoritism shown to foreigners quickly lost him the goodwill of the people. When Godwin returned in 1052 with his sons and an army, the English people were willing to support him. Edward retained his position, but he had to take his wife back and restore all of the Godwin lands to the family.

The following year, 1053, Godwin died, and his son, Harold, began to take the place of his father, particularly when it came to keeping control of the people. Harold was not a part of the royal succession as he was not a blood relative to Edward; however, Edward never had children with his wife (Harold's sister). For years, it is said that Edward would hold the line of succession out to people to get what he wanted or needed. With no clear successor, it would have certainly been a very powerful bargaining chip for a man who was not popular with the people he ruled.

Harold proved that he was a capable leader, finally forcing Wales to submit to English rule and also negotiating a peace with the Northumbrians. All of this he did between 1063 and 1065. Despite his strength as a leader, the next person in line to the throne was the Duke of Normandy, William, more commonly known in history as William the Conqueror. As Edward's cousin, he had a much stronger claim to the throne, and some historians believe that Edward actually promised the throne to William.

When he was dying, Edward finally gave his decision as to who he wanted as his successor, and he named Harold. Edward's childless marriage would later come to be seen as a sign of just how pious he was, earning him a sainthood and the name Edward the Confessor. Some believe he was an ineffective ruler, while others believe that he was shrewd and knew his own limitations. As king, the only power that he insisted on retaining was in naming the bishops; most of the other power of his position was exercised by Godwin for most of Edward's reign. When Edward died, he left a power vacuum that would not be resolved peacefully. A new king, Harold, reigning as Harold II, was crowned the next day, but that did not resolve the question of who was the rightful heir to the throne.

Harold had the support of many of the people of England because he was the son to the beloved Godwin and the victor over so many problematic factions on the island. Some say that before Edward's death, Harold had even traveled to visit William to swear an oath of fealty and to support William's ascension. Whether Harold did this willingly, was forced to, or whether the exchange never happened is uncertain as the people who described it were the Normans, William's people.

Harold may have had the support of many people, but William controlled many of the vital harbors between Schelde and Brest. He sought the blessing from the pope (and received it) to attack England to claim his rightful place. With recruits from all over continental Europe, William was able to establish considerable military strength. He was also an excellent military strategist and likely implemented his own type of discipline on the soldiers from so many different nations (including France, Spain, Flanders, and Italy).

It was not easy to attack England because the winds had to be right to make the passage (as the Spanish Armada would learn when they tried to remove Elizabeth I from power in the 16th century). William was more knowledgeable about the potential sailing troubles, and after a difficult start, he finally had the desirable conditions to safely cross the English Channel.

Upon learning of William's arrival in Sussex, Harold quickly amassed as many men as he could and headed to face the invaders. This would prove to be a valiant and daring move that failed. Harold could have waited for more men who were trained instead of adding peasants and other untrained soldiers to his army. It is probable that he hoped to quickly beat William back into the channel where the environment could have done a considerable amount of damage to the Norman army. Harold had about 7,000 men to William's 4,000 to 7,000. The difference was really in the training that the soldiers had, and in that, William had the upper hand.

As soon as William learned of Harold's actions, he rounded up his men to meet Harold in battle. William's strategy was well planned, and he structured the advance in a way that worked best for each of the division's strengths. As was the usual practice at the time, the archers led, and the heavy infantry followed directly behind them with the knights marching behind them. The left side of the army was made up of the Bretons, and on the right were the French, giving the men of other countries the ability to work together during the battle.

Harold had only two choices from the ridge he occupied just northwest of Hastings. Instead of retreating, Harold chose to stand and fight. He organized his soldiers as best he could, but the ridge was not well suited to the task, and he suffered heavy casualties from the beginning.

Things did not go easily for William's forces either. The archers were an easy target from their position at the bottom of the ridge, and many of them died before William sent his cavalry to attack Harold's forces. They faced a large horde of infantry carrying very effective two-handed battle-axes. Many of those who were not immediately cut down panicked. William acted to check those who were trying to leave the field and took on the English who followed them. He would lure more of Harold's forces out over the course of the battle by pretending to retreat. This feint proved very effective, and he was able to kill or wound a large number of English soldiers.

Both of Harold's brothers were killed during the battle, and Harold fell later in the day. The English continued their struggle against William's forces until night fell. Under the darkness of the night, the English left the field, retreating to their homes.

In a single day, the largest problem of the succession that had plagued the island was much closer to being resolved. William would be crowned a couple of months later on December 25, 1066.

This was not the first nor the last time that the succession would be questioned in England. This nation has a long and storied history with the kind of intrigues that are associated with the position of ruler. While monarchs of other nations would face similar problems, no other European country seems to have been as contentious over determining who would be the ruler as in England. Still, the Battle of Hastings stands out among those quests for power, as years of fighting between the two men most likely to take the throne was resolved in a single day. The battle removed the next king chosen by Edward the Confessor and made it easier for one of his blood relatives to ascend the throne.

The Anarchy

The history of the English throne is long and bloody, with the Battle of Hastings being only one of many instances where two sides would claim to have been granted the kingdom following the death of a childless king. The Anarchy is very different in that King Henry I had two children, a son and a daughter. While succession usually went to a male heir, Henry I was adamant that his daughter had an equal claim to the throne should he die.

Henry I's daughter Adelaide was born in 1102, and his son William was born the next year. When she was just 10 or 11 years old, Adelaide was married to the Holy Roman Emperor Henry V, who was 20 years older than her. Following their marriage, her name was changed to Matilda. Over the next few decades, she watched as her husband put down revolts and dealt with the power struggles of the vast empire. By the time he died in 1125, she had learned a lot about retaining control over an empire and negotiating with many different factions. Any children that she and Henry V had did not survive to adulthood, so when he died, his nephew became the new emperor.

Her father, Henry I, knew that his lineage was in danger because he had no legitimate sons to take his place. His son and heir, William, had died in the *White Ship* disaster in 1120, leaving him with no other obvious heir. With his daughter now a widower, he saw the opportunity to solidify his lineage once it became obvious that he would not have another son, so Henry I summoned Matilda back to Normandy. Knowing that many of the noblemen would not want to support a queen, Henry I had all of the nobles come to Westminster where they swore that they would accept and support Matilda as queen following Henry I's death. Any children she would have would follow her in the line of succession.

The obvious problem was that she was unmarried, which greatly reduced her appeal. If she were to die without children, accepting her would only put off the inevitable fight for the throne. Henry I knew this, and in 1128, he selected her second husband, Geoffrey V, the Count of Anjou, who was 15 years old (10 years younger than her). They would have a son five years later, and they named him Henry. Matilda had a second son the next year, and he was named Geoffrey.

Henry I died the following year, 1135. The problem that he had anticipated soon came to pass, and the members of the nobility who had sworn to support Matilda soon turned to Stephen of Blois as their king. Stephen claimed that Henry I had changed his mind on his deathbed and had made him the heir. Considering the events that Henry I had organized to ensure that Matilda would be next in line to the throne, it is obvious that Stephen was just looking to take the throne as the closest male heir. Many of the nobles did not want to be ruled by a woman, especially one who had spent most of her life living with a family that many Englishmen felt was their enemy. They welcomed the coup, ignoring their pledges and oaths because they wanted to have a king instead of a queen.

Matilda and Geoffrey were not entirely surprised by the move, and soon after Henry I died, they began to ensure they had control of the castles in Normandy (part of today's northern France, but it was part of England during much of the Middle Ages). They likely did not make the trek across the English Channel because she was pregnant when her father died. The rebelling noblemen had Stephen crowned king before a month had passed after Henry I's death.

There were some who remembered their oaths, and they almost immediately took up their banners for Matilda. The first notable battle occurred when David I, King of Scotland (and a relative of Matilda's Scottish mother), attacked the English from the north.

Matilda's half-brother, Robert of Gloucester (born to a mistress of Henry I and as an illegitimate son had no legitimate claim to the throne), took up arms in 1138, revolting against the usurper king. It was his declaration of war that began a civil war in England. Around this time, David I was defeated, and he made peace with Stephen. However, others were now fighting on Matilda's behalf.

In 1139, Matilda and Geoffrey arrived in England to have her take her rightful place as queen. Robert of Gloucester proved to be an asset, and he helped her to quickly take the southwestern portion of the island. Over the next 12 years, both Stephen and Matilda would be captured, but they would either be released or escaped (Matilda escaped twice, while Stephen was released by Matilda in exchange for her Robert, who had also been captured). Robert of Gloucester was killed during one of the battles in 1147, and Matilda's eldest son, Henry, soon became the leader of those who supported Matilda (he had joined the war in 1142 when he was 11 years old). His first assault against Stephen proved that he had too little experience as a military leader, as he had hired too few mercenaries and was easily defeated by Stephen's men. It did not help that Henry did not have the financial means to pay the mercenaries back, and his mother refused to cover the payments.

Matilda's husband Geoffrey died in 1151. Henry would again try to take the throne in 1153 and met with greater success than his first attempt, but he did not manage to win any decisive victories. Tired of the civil war, the Church stepped in to mediate between Henry and Stephen. An agreement was reached that made Henry the successor to the throne once Stephen died. This actually happened the following year, and on the same day, Henry was crowned Henry II.

Matilda was never granted her birthright, as she was noticeably passed over for a king who had a flimsy claim to the throne. Some point to her haughty attitude and her foreign connections as the reason why she could not gain supporters. This may have been a contributing factor, but as many men have proven, they did not need to be well liked to be king (as can be seen with King John in the next century). The problem was that she was a woman, and the men of the nation did not want to be ruled by one. This was a lesson that future English queens would study and learn from. None would learn how to deal with men like Queen Elizabeth I, who would usher England into a golden age several centuries later.

The Magna Carta – 1215

Part of the reason why England became so much stronger than other European nations is that it divided power among several people instead of having it all consolidated under a single ruler and his offspring. This power dynamic would certainly change significantly throughout the Middle Ages, but the members of the nobility and people outside of the royal family were guaranteed a degree of say in the direction of the country because of the Magna Carta.

Long after the Battle of Hastings established Norman rule over England, the nation would go through more difficulties because of the Crusades. William the Conqueror had ensured that his descendants would rule over the country, and he amassed considerable power during his reign. He forced the people to obey him, stripping many of them of the power that they had held under Edward and Harold. He was a jealous ruler who would not allow anyone to question his authority. Even the pope was only allowed minor control over the religious workings in England. Some of this authority was lost under Henry I, who had to relinquish some of the power back to the noblemen. Following generations would guarantee some level of power to the nobles, but the king would still retain most of the control over all aspects of the government and church. Laws were rewritten and reworked to reflect changes in the common law.

Over time, some kings would have little interest in ruling over England, as was the case with Richard I, known as Richard the Lionheart. He spent much of his time fighting in the Crusades, and he often warred with France. Following his death, his brother John became king in 1199. The notorious King John (the villain of most Robin Hood stories) was left with a messy situation and financial problems because of his late brother's constant wars. The nobles and people were already unhappy, but they did not want to blame the late king. John was a much easier target as he was not as affable. He almost immediately made the nobles uncomfortable because he broke a tradition that had started after William I's death where kings would issue charters to the barons after ascending the throne. King John failed to do this, creating tension very early in his reign. In an attempt to placate the restless barons, two of John's advisors spoke on the king's behalf, saying that the barons would retain their rights if they were faithful to the new king.

By 1201, the barons refused to further support John without his acknowledgment of their rights. In 1205, this became a serious problem for John as the French began to invade and he had too few men to support him. Things continued to go poorly for John as taxes were either not paid or were insufficient to sustain efforts against enemies on many fronts. In addition to the French, he had a contentious relationship with Pope Innocent III, who had Stephen Langton elected to the position of Archbishop of Canterbury. John had wanted another person to take over as archbishop. In fact, King John had wanted John de Grey, the Bishop of Norwich, to become the next archbishop, and the monks in Canterbury chose someone else. The pope ignored both, resulting in Stephen Langton's election. In 1209, the pope excommunicated John over the quarrel. When John relented, it is no surprise that Langton emerged as a voice against the king.

King John was finally put in a position where he had few allies. Langton and several members of the nobility saw this as an opportunity to avoid war by having the king and the rebelling nobles sit down to negotiate a longer-term solution. The result was the Articles of the Barons, which would come to be the first draft of what would one day be the Magna Carta. King John accepted the final version in June of 1215. It showed that John understood his position well enough, and he did not want to see a civil war break out in England. This was his way of stopping the bloodshed of his people for a war that would have no winners.

The Magna Carta would be reissued or confirmed several more times (1216, 1217, 1225, 1237, 1253, and 1297) to ensure that the barons continued to support the king. Outside forces constantly sought to take control of the island, particularly France. By reissuing the document, kings earned the loyalty of their people who would stand to lose much more by supporting the invaders who were not likely to follow the terms of the document.

The primary purpose of the Magna Carta was to ensure the rights and control of the nobility. One of the most notable guarantees under the Magna Carta dealt with free men: "No man shall be arrested or imprisoned, except by the judgement of their equals and by the law of the land." Notice that this only applied to freemen and not to the vast majority of the people in England. Peasants were considered the property of the people who owned the land so it would not apply to them, and the lords and nobles could continue to imprison the peasants for no reason.

However, the line does play an important role when it comes to holding leaders accountable. Under this line of the Magna Carta, even the king could be held to account for any wrongdoings against the free people. It was the first time where a king could be held responsible for infringing on the rights of others. This would become a cornerstone of many nations around the world. Both Thomas Jefferson and Mahatma Gandhi would use it as the foundation for the governments they would help establish.

Chapter 9 – The Hundred Years' War – 1337 to 1453

Less than 50 years after the Church-sanctioned Crusades finally ceased, European countries began to turn on each other. None of the ensuing European wars were as heated or as lengthy as the war over the French succession. The start of the war was similar to the war over succession in England because the king of France, Charles IV, had failed to produce an heir, which left relatives and close advisors to fight over who was the next rightful king.

Questions of succession often caused bloodshed as people sought more power or to have what they felt was rightfully theirs. It was dangerous for a king to die without a son because war was all but inevitable afterward. The Hundred Years' War was no different.

Of course, with the dates of the war going from 1337 to 1453, the war actually lasted almost 120 years. The name was given to the war by historians of the 1800s, and that name has not been protested. Since the fighting did periodically stop, the war was not continuous, making the Hundred Years' War an easy name to remember, if not entirely accurate.

The Connection Between France and England

France and England were closely connected during the Middles Ages, both by marriage and by their geographical proximity. Parts of what is now northern France belonged to England during much of the Middle Ages because of the intermarrying between the royal families, giving England a foothold on the continent.

William the Conqueror spent much of his life in Normandy prior to taking the English throne from Harold II at the Battle of Hastings. Those who followed William expanded the English claim on the continent. The most notable was Henry II who inherited Anjou from his father Geoffrey and further increased the claim by marrying Eleanor of Aquitaine. The French kings were not pleased with the amount of land that was being converted into English territory, and conflicts did occasionally arise.

It did not help that Eleanor divorced the French King Louis VII and married Henry II before he became king. Her lands were located in southern France, which meant that England then had a foothold on both sides of the country. Eleanor went on to help rule England when her son Richard I went off to the Crusades. His brother, the wildly unpopular King John, did not rely on his mother as Richard I had, and she mostly dealt with managing Aquitaine after John ascended the throne. Perhaps his rule would be better remembered if he had involved her more in the administration of England as she was obviously a more capable ruler and manager of affairs than her youngest son.

In addition to being pressed to sign the Magna Carta, King John also lost much of the lands that his father had controlled in failed campaigns. The largest lands that he lost were Anjou and Normandy, though there were other regions that were returned to France under his rule. Aquitaine would switch hands over the next century, with both France and England fighting for the wealthy area on the continent.

Both countries had enemies in surrounding countries, and whenever one country was distracted by warring with other nations, the other country would slip in and take lands for itself. This constant fighting over the same regions would finally erupt in a full-scale war.

A Question of Succession

The Hundred Years' War had its origins in uncertainty about the next rightful king. When Charles IV died in 1328, he left no obvious heir to the French throne. Edward III of England was the nephew of Charles IV, whose mother was Isabella of France, Charles' sister. She claimed the throne for Edward III, but the nobles of France refused to allow the English king (then only 15 years old) to take control of their country. By citing an obscure Salic law and an old Frankish law, they said that no succession could pass through a female. The next closest male to the throne through only male inheritance was Philip of Valois, who became Philip VI.

At the time, Edward III had only been the English king for a year, and it was his mother and her lover, Roger Mortimer, who ruled the country after deposing his father, Edward II. Edward III perhaps learned how to be ruthless from his mother, as he would go on to have Mortimer executed in 1330. He chose to banish his mother though. Neither Isabella nor Mortimer had pressed Edward III's claim to the French throne, something that he seemed interested in pursuing now, if for no other reason than as a way of negotiating with Philip VI for the disputed territories. The English king, however, did not seriously seek to stake his claim to the throne until Philip VI provoked him.

France Takes Aquitaine

Edward III of England was busy fighting against David II, King of Scotland, during the early years of the 14th century. France saw two opportunities. First, they provided support to the Scottish king, further eroding their relationship with England. When England began to turn its attention to the French aggression, King Philip VI took Aquitaine in 1337. This was the action that initiated the Hundred Years' War, which raged on and off for more than 100 years.

In response to Philip VI's clear theft of English lands, Edward III decided to stake his rightful claim to the throne. Considering the fact that he was a closer descendant to the previous kings and obscure laws had been used to omit his claim, he had a very strong claim against Philip VI as a usurper to the throne.

A War on Several Fronts

Just as Philip VI had supported Edward III's enemy, David II, Edward III looked to Philip VI's enemies and the nobles who were discontented with his reign. Edward III was an adept politician, and he fanned the flames among some of the nobles who then turned on Philip VI.

Edward III's strength was in his fighting abilities though. He brought English nobles who joined with the Frenchmen who sided with Edward III, and they plundered many lands, creating a serious problem for the French king. The French attempted similar plundering on British soil, but the English navy was stronger and better prepared. For most of the early years, much of the fighting was conducted through raids instead of all-out war.

There were two notable battles, Crécy and Poitiers, that showed just how much more capable the English were on the field. During the battle at Poitiers, Philip VI was captured. With Edward III's raiding parties causing issues across other areas of France, it was all but impossible for the now leaderless France to withstand the English army. By this point, Edward III's eldest son, Edward, later known as the Black Prince, joined the war. Edward would be called the Black Prince after his death because of his ruthless efficiency in battle (some say that he wore black armor which could also be the reason for his name). He was one of Edward III's greatest military strategists and was one of the reasons for the English king's victories. Though Philip died in 1350, Edward III would continue to fight for the French throne.

Edward III and his son pressed close to Paris but could not successfully take control of the capital. In 1360, Edward III signed the Treaty of Brétigny. He would no longer seek his claim to the throne as long as France recognized that Aquitaine was English and paid him a large sum of money. This should have been the end of the war, but poor wording (or perhaps intentionally misleading wording) made it possible for both England and France to argue that things were not fully settled.

France tried to take Aquitaine just nine years later under Charles V. Large battles were again avoided, but France was able to make gains during this time. The Black Prince had assisted King Pedro to restore him to his throne in Castile in 1366. Many believe that he contracted an illness during his time in Spain that he never fully recovered from, dying in 1376. Edward III died the next year, but he had been unable to do much fighting in his later years. Upon Edward III's death, Richard II, the Black Prince's son, became the next English king. England was not as fully invested in the war as they had been, but they still fought for roughly a decade.

When Charles V of France died in 1380, along with his staunch supporter Bertrand du Guesclin, neither France nor England wanted to carry on the war started by dead rulers. Skirmishes and raiding continued, but there were no large battles for a while. Once Richard II was old enough to rule (he was 10 when he became king), he sought peace. The new French king, Charles VI, was more interested in joining the Crusades than in continuing the war, so a tentative peace was reached.

Richard II proved to be an unpopular king, with his people considering him to be too much of a tyrant, and he was deposed in

1399. Charles VI did not fare much better as he started to show signs of insanity by 1392. His first bout of the illness caused him to fly into a rage and kill four of his knights and then nearly kill Louis I, his brother and the Duke of Orléans.

The war resumed at the beginning of the 15th century, but this time it was driven by French nobles vying for the power available because their king was insane. Two primary factions were created, the Orléans and the Burgundians. When civil war broke out in France in 1407, the English king Henry V saw his chance to reclaim the lands lost during the latter part of the previous century and signed a treaty with some of the French nobles. Following a tentative peace between the French nobles, Henry V attacked. One of the most famous battles in English and French history occurred at Agincourt in 1415 (near Crécy where Edward III had earned a significant victory against France at the start of the war). As Henry V's first campaign in this long war, it proved to many that he was a very capable military leader. Because of his decisive victory against the French, members of the nobility and leaders of other nations were willing to back him in his pursuit of French lands.

The French nobles were still fighting with each other, and talks to ally against Henry V resulted in further bloodshed instead of peace. Finally, the leader of the Burgundy faction made a deal with Henry V, and in 1420, his negotiations with Henry V resulted in the Treaty of Troyes. Henry V married the daughter of the mad king, Catherine of Valois, meaning he would be the heir to the French throne. Henry V continued the war but only against Louis I, Duke of Orléans and the current Dauphin, or heir to the throne. How this would have played out will never be known as Henry V did not live to see the end of the fighting. He died in 1422, and Charles VI died soon after him, removing the primary power struggle between the two French noble sides.

The next in line for the English throne was Henry VI, who was not yet a year old. Regents served as the rulers of England while the infant grew up. They continued the fighting, but the alliance with the Burgundians was no longer as strong as it had been under Henry V.

The Rise of an Unlikely French Hero – Joan of Arc

France had been fighting within itself and against England for over 80 years. The peasants had been through famine, the Black Death, and constant raids by English soldiers and mercenaries who were not loyal to any side. The constant fighting took the biggest toll on them, and it was from their lowly ranks that a new force would arise.

Up until this point, England had been the stronger country; although they had lost a considerable amount of land, they were resilient. The division between the noble families in France only strengthened the English.

Born around 1412 to peasants, Joan of Arc was not considered as being anyone important during much of her early life. Her family had nothing, and because of her gender, she shouldn't have had the ability to better her opportunities for the future. Regardless, Joan found power in the voices and visions that she claimed to have by the time she was 13 years old. According to her, the visions showed her how to assist the men who were fighting for the recognition of Charles VII, the son of Charles VI, as the rightful king of France instead of Henry VI. By this point, England had taken Paris, leaving the Dauphin Charles to find a new home. He established his court in Chinon, France.

Joan went to Vaucoulers in 1428 to petition Robert de Baudricourt, the garrison commander of the town, for an armed escort to see the Dauphin. Her request was denied. Joan of Arc waited a full year, during which time France made no progress in their struggles. When she came back, she made a prediction that actually came true, and Robert de Baudricourt granted her an escort. Upon meeting Charles VII, she told him that she was meant to fight against the English and the end result would be that he would be crowned king at Reims. Charles decided to trust her and the voices she claimed to hear, and she was placed in the thick of the fighting at Orléans.

Her visions appeared to be real in the beginning. Dressed as a fighter, she helped bring the first real victory for France when they drove the English out of Orléans. This heartened the French, and they began to experience more victories, with Joan among the leaders. Soon after, Charles was crowned King Charles VII in Reims, just as Joan had promised. Her leadership soon turned though, and she was captured in 1430 just outside of France. She was taken prisoner by the Burgundians, but they had no issue with turning her over to the English. Ecstatic about her capture, the English vilified her, calling her a witch. Both the Burgundians and the English tried to say that her capture proved she was not following divine instructions, and since Charles VII had been using her to obtain victory, it proved that he was following a diabolical woman, which invalidated his coronation. To prove that she was not protected by any divine being, the English burned her at the stake in 1431 under the charge of crossdressing, which she did to maintain her virtue. Unlike the treatment of the men they captured, the English established a smear campaign against Joan to discredit any good she had done for France. In some cases, men who had accomplished similar victories had even been begrudgingly respected for their ability to pull themselves up from nothing to become a capable military leader.

The Orléans victory because of Joan led to the nobles of Burgundy switching their allegiance to the French king instead of the English. By 1435, the English had very little chance of winning back the lands that they had once claimed. They were also embroiled in their own issues with succession back home, which meant they did not have the energy or resources to expend on trying to keep their dwindling claims on the continent. The war dragged on for almost another 20 years, but it did not see the same voracity as it had during the beginning or the period following the madness of Charles VI. In

1455, the English civil war known as the War of the Roses would begin, ending any interest they had in trying to claim the French throne.

The war and the reasons for it had evolved over the 120 years it lasted. However, it was the culmination of several problems that had finally sparked the war. When the Hundred Years' War finally ended, England no longer retained any land on the continent or any claim to the French throne.

Among the most notable changes brought about because of the war were advances in science and weaponry. The continent moved from the Middle Ages into the early modern period while England and France fought over territory. Knights became all but obsolete by the end of the war, and guns had been introduced into the European military landscape. Military strategies and organization also changed significantly, with many countries adopting standing armies instead of relying on peasants who were untrained.

Chapter 10 – The Horrors of Nature

The Middles Ages was plagued by war and fighting as people began to find their own national identities, argued over religion, and fought over control. However, war was hardly the only concern for the people of Europe. Even during times of peace, peasants struggled to survive. They had little control over their fates and little opportunity to better their situations.

Nature proved to be just as cruel to them as any of the lords, kings, popes, and emperors who came to power during the Middle Ages. The two most poignant examples of nature proving more powerful than people came in the form of famine and plague.

The Great Famine of 1315-1317

The Great Famine of 1315-1317 is still remembered and discussed today in the areas that were affected. Even more than 700 years after it ended, most of the people in the Western world have heard of it, although most people cannot tell you much about it.

Throughout most of the Middle Ages, agriculture improved and people were increasingly able to sustain their numbers with less concern about daily survival than they had during the period right after Rome fell. The improvements in farming techniques and equipment up until the 14th century allowed much of Western Europe to grow and expand. By 1315, the population was robust, and the amount of food produced was just barely able to keep up with the booming population. For several decades, the conditions for growing food and managing livestock were ideal, making it appear that everything was perfectly fine. However, the continent reached a tipping point. If the weather conditions varied, thereby stalling or reducing food production, there would not be enough adequate resources to provide for the population of most areas.

Famines were not new to Europe; they had managed to get through them over the history of the continent, just like every other major civilization. However, the difference was that Europe had never had such a large population prior to 1315. Despite the constant wars and Crusades, Europeans were having more children, and those children were surviving longer. This is what made the Great Famine so devastating. Food production managed to keep up with the growing population, but it did not leave much room for any mishaps or problems at any stage of the production process.

A contributing factor to the problems was the shift in climate. Spring became increasingly longer and wetter than in previous centuries. Rains continued to fall well into summer, making it a cooler season, and fall started earlier. This meant that the growing season became increasingly shorter.

The spring of 1315 ended up having far more precipitation than normal, creating conditions that were too wet for farmers and peasants to sow seeds properly. Not only that, but they were also unable to plow all of the areas dedicated to growing food because of the constant rains. Since the rains did not stop, some of the seeds rotted in the ground instead of sprouting.

With these smaller crop yields, people realized they did not have enough adequate food to last over the cold winter. Hoping to supplement the lost crops, they journeyed into the forests to find food. The increase of people foraging in the forests quickly left little food in them. Some forests in certain countries were also part of nobles' lands, and poaching on them was illegal, reducing how much food the people were able to acquire. Punishment for poaching varied, though people would risk punishment over starving to death.

Records indicate that there were not many deaths at the start of the Great Famine. The problem was that when spring arrived in 1316, the peasants were weakened after being malnourished over the winter. This meant that they were able to plow less than the previous spring and were unable to make up for the previous year. The winter of 1316 was brutal, and some families left children in the forest to die (giving rise to stories like "Hansel and Gretel") because they could not feed the whole family. Some older members of the family opted to starve instead of taking food from the younger family members.

By 1317, even the nobles and monarchs felt the effects of the Great Famine, though to a much lesser degree than the peasants. After two years of living with too little food, the peasants did not have the ability to make the most out of the return to more typical spring weather. The problem was compounded because there were fewer seeds to start the harvest. Since less food had been produced over the last two years, people resorted to eating the seeds to stay alive when the food ran out.

The people were also more susceptible to illness. It is estimated that between 10 and 15 percent of the population died from illnesses like tuberculosis, pneumonia, and bronchitis. It is tragically ironic that the large culling of the population was what helped contribute to the recovery from the Great Famine. With fewer people to feed, less food was required to be grown.

If the Great Famine was a sign, it should have been considered as a warning to the people of Europe. What followed it was far more deadly, and there was no known cure for it like there was for hunger.

The Black Death

The growth of the population was dangerous for Europe not only because of food production. People were not equipped to deal with the living conditions that arose from the rapid growth of towns and small cities. Some peasants were able to leave the feudal system to seek better opportunities, but many of them were attracted to the growing areas, resulting in the growth of towns as population hubs. With most of Europe not having had any experience with such a large population, people lived in fairly unhygienic, cramped conditions.

There were rumors of a lethal disease spreading across Asia and the Near East brought by travelers of the Silk Road and sailors. To most Europeans, the rumors seemed like a concern that did not apply to them. Some believed that the problem was too far away and could not possibly be a risk to Europe. Others felt that it was a punishment to the believers in heathen religions for not believing in the Christian god. In 1347, they were all to be proven wrong.

It is likely that the plague arrived in multiple places as it was spreading across the known world, including ports and areas where Europeans traveled. The ports of Italy were the first to experience the plague firsthand in Europe. Considering how fast the disease worked (you could be healthy one morning and dead a week later), the sources of the plague must have been relatively close.

The most well-known method for spreading the plague was through a flea bite. Considering the hygiene of the time, this certainly could have been a contributing factor. The problem was that fleas were not the only method of spreading the disease. Fleas passed on the bubonic strain of the plague, but it was also possible to contract it from someone suffering from the pneumonic (respiratory) plague. The third type of plague is septicemic, which infects the blood. The biggest problem was that a person who had any version of the plague was likely to have two or all three types of the plague by the time they died. People infected by fleas had a 40% survival rate. It is estimated that between a quarter and a third of the population of Europe died because of the plague, with survival being extremely rare. Naturally, the people had no idea what was spreading the plague, so they took many different measures to try to survive.

Rats, mice, and other animals certainly contributed to the spread of the plague, but the living conditions were equally significant in the spread of the disease. People were living in smaller buildings, closer together. This was the ideal condition for the spread of the pneumonic plague since anyone who breathed in the air particles near someone with this form of the plague would almost certainly become ill and die. The mortality rate for someone with the pneumonic plague was nearly 100%, as was septicemic plague (though this was not nearly so easily transmitted as the pneumonic plague).

The plague spread from the port cities along trade routes, through towns and cities, and across the continent in about a year's time. It did not discriminate, taking peasants, rulers, clergy, and merchants. Edward III's daughter, Princess Joan, was on her way to marry a prince of Spain. Members of her wedding party fell ill with the plague after they reached Bordeaux. She died less than a month after her arrival, potentially changing the entire political structure of Europe. Her marriage to the son of King Alfonso XI of Castile would have created a strong bond between England and Spain. The French already had problems with both countries, but the marriage could have compounded the problem. With the death of Princess Joan, Edward III and the Black Prince put aside fighting and went to a place that was safer than the populated cities to survive.

The plague would return periodically over the next few hundred years, although it was not nearly as deadly after its initial arrival. Cities had learned to quarantine potentially contaminated travelers and to keep anyone potentially affected from entering and mixing with the general population (though they did not know what caused the plague for several more centuries).

This pandemic would later be called the Black Death, and it left an immense scar on the psyche of Europeans. Even today, the Western world has only a basic understanding of what happened and how it affected the path of Europe in the ages that were to come.

Both the Great Famine and the Black Death occurred around the time that the Middle Ages were ending and the early modern era began. This is in large part because they played a significant role in causing people to question all forms of authority, including the Catholic Church (which had been unable to do anything to stop or alleviate the suffering during either crisis), and in forcing people to begin to think in terms of their own protection and safety. The requirements for survival were shifting as the continent began to move away from being predominately agrarian. Being forced to think for themselves, the people of Europe began to change. Each disaster was probably a contributing factor to the thought processes and examination of humanity that would result in the Renaissance by the end of the 14th century.

Chapter 11 – Higher Education and The Gothic Period – How the Middle Ages Advanced Education and Architecture

Perhaps the most compelling argument that the Middle Ages weren't the Dark Ages they are so often called is that during this time the concept of universities was born. While there is no argument that Europe saw a decline in many of the sciences and mathematics, that did not mean that the people were completely unenlightened or that they did not value education.

The social structure during the Middle Ages was not significantly different than during the Roman Empire, and the status of peasants did not significantly change. Wars, raids, and skirmishes certainly affected the peasants often, but even these battles had been a problem as the Roman Empire shrank. During the Middle Ages, food production became easier, and the population began to grow much faster than at any other point in European history. More opportunities became available as serfs and peasants were able to leave their homes and move to new areas. The rise of towns meant that other skills were needed to meet the demands of the more densely populated areas and the people who lived there.

The Middle Ages also saw the rise of an entirely new kind of architecture that is just as famous and breathtaking as any of the architecture that the ancient Greeks and Romans accomplished. In addition to these large, magnificent buildings, education began to be offered to people who did not have power and status, though it was primarily offered to those who were willing to dedicate their lives to the Church.

Finally, some of the most influential minds helped establish a new direction for the continent. Much of their work reflected strong ties to religion, but those works have proven to be far more universal in their appeal, even today. The literary works and philosophies of this time permeate the European mentality, and those same works are still just as well known today (perhaps even better today with the higher literacy rate and the Internet) as they were in their own time.

The Start of Higher Education in Europe

The Romans were not interested in educating people who were below a certain rank. Their great philosophers, artists, and writers focused on a few groups, but for the most part, they did not care about the masses. People who lived far from Rome were considered barbaric, and they were not considered intelligent or cultured enough to be able to understand the finer parts of Roman life.

This was not true of the pious people of the Middle Ages. There are letters from merchants, innkeepers, and other people of the lower classes to prove that the literacy rate was not as low as many people believe. Serfs and many peasants probably could not read or write, but others were not barred from learning.

There was a push during the Middle Ages to start to provide education for more than just the elite or a few specific classes of people. People in the clergy could generally read and write, and they saw the benefit in helping to educate the people under their religious care. Like shepherds with a flock, they wanted to give them guidance that would improve their lives.

Over time, the lessons carried out at monasteries, churches, and convents came to resemble institutions of higher education. As time passed, monasteries became dedicated to providing basic education for their students. Of course, not everyone could attend. Those who were part of the feudal system or whose jobs required them to be in the fields or traveling were unable to attend. However, monasteries tended to welcome anyone who was interested in learning about general subjects, including reading and writing.

With many of the greatest leaders of the Middle Ages coming from a much wider range of situations, the Church had a much better understanding of the potential of its people (something it would forget by the early modern era as it fought to keep control). Cathedrals became the place where people could go for further lessons after completing their education at local religious centers. In this new environment, secondary education began to grow and flourish. Students who could attend the classes at cathedrals and their associated schools could learn more about the arts, humanities, law, and medicine, depending on where their interests lay and if the school had a specialization.

Europe's two oldest universities began during this time: the University of Bologna (1088) and the University of Paris (1150). The University of Paris today is divided into more than a dozen universities, but the University of Bologna continues to be one of the most prestigious universities today, with an estimated 80,000 to 90,000 students. England followed suit a century after Paris, with the founding of the Universities of Oxford and Cambridge.

It was the University of Bologna that first named schools for higher education. The name is derived from the Latin word "universitas." The Latin term refers to a group of people who are united as one body, a community, society, or corporation, and it was not originally intended to be applied specifically to education. Higher education was a concept that began in the Middle Ages. There may not have been as much progress in math and science during the Middle Ages, but they began to share knowledge with a much wider group of people.

Astounding Architectural Achievements

The architecture of the Middle Ages was completely unique and is frequently imitated today, and it is known as Gothic architecture. The beginnings of this architecture began in the early 11th century, but it was not an established style that was imitated until the early 1200s.

The earliest buildings that reflect several different aspects of the Gothic style appeared in France around the middle of the 12th century, as builders and architects were drawing inspiration from some of the structures of the previous century. England began to experiment with the Gothic style soon after its appearance in France. Among the most notable buildings still standing of this style of architecture are Westminster Abbey, Canterbury Cathedral, Sainte-Chapelle, and Notre Dame.

The Gothic style was primarily used for churches, monasteries, and other buildings related to Christianity. There were smaller churches and private builders that began to adapt the style over the next few hundred years. One can easily recognize buildings in the Gothic style because there is nothing subtle about them. Their spires stretch up, making them easy to see from a distance. Gargoyles were remarkable additions that provided a very somber feel to these structures, enhancing the flying buttresses and pointed arches that still attract the eye today.

Stained glass windows are one of the most intriguing elements of Gothic architecture. The buildings themselves may appear to very solemn, but the addition of stained glass makes them far brighter and colorful on the inside. The effort to construct these windows is very complex, showing just how dedicated and ingenious the skilled workers of the time were.

Another thing to note was just how difficult it would have been to construct these immense buildings with the tools of the Middle Ages. People are often in awe of the Egyptian pyramids, but they follow a fairly rigid structure that offers a stronger foundation. By comparison, the Gothic style has many additions that at first glance are completely impractical. Although math and science were not nearly as important to most of the people of the Middle Ages, Gothic architecture proves that those who understood math did continue to push the boundaries, working to defy reason by creating magnificent structures that are still mind-boggling today. Also, consider the fact that these buildings were made almost entirely of stone and not the lighter materials of today. These buildings have managed to withstand an uncountable number of wars and battles, as well as centuries that have brought down newer structures that were not nearly so sturdy or impressive.

Brilliant Minds of the Middle Ages

The arts of the Middle Ages were unique, with the most impressive visual art of the time easily being the enormous Gothic structures. Similarly, some of the greatest works in literature still tower over the works that have come since. Most people could not name any works of literature from the Renaissance and the next few centuries, but virtually everyone in the west has heard of the stories written by the most notable writers of the Middle Ages. Part of this can be attributed to the writers of the Renaissance and later periods focusing more on math, philosophy, and science over stories. Still, the stories of the Middle Ages have universal themes and are so well written that they can still be related to today (even if the backdrop is foreign to modern audiences).

One of the largest figures to come out of the Middle Ages actually is well known today because of his exploits and not because of his writing. Marco Polo (1254-1324) was a merchant who constantly traveled the Silk Road taking European goods to Asia and returning with Asian goods to sell. He interacted with Kublai Khan, working as one of his envoys. He fought with the Venetians against the Genoese and was captured. During the year he was imprisoned by the Genoese, he told his story to one of the other prisoners, Rustichello da Pisa, who wrote it down. It was a biography of his exploration of far-off countries, particularly China and Japan. There are still original copies of the story of his life that exist in Europe, such as the copy in the Paris library and in Berne. His story went on to inspire men like Christopher Columbus (another Italian) who helped start the Age of Discovery during the early modern era.

Thomas Aquinas (1225-1274) was one of the most well-known figures of the time. He was a prolific writer about theology and humanity, and he constantly sought ways to improve the human condition and soul. During a time when the emphasis was on religion and the Christian god, he wrote about them in relation to metaphysics, logic, psychology (long before it was an established science), philosophy, language, politics, and ethics. His most famous work was the proof of the Christian god's existence, and many of his writings are the foundation for the beliefs of the Roman Catholic Church today. Despite people considering the Middle Ages as a period devoid of philosophy, Thomas Aquinas is considered one of the ten most influential philosophers in Western history.

Geoffrey Chaucer (c. 1343-1400) is easily one of the most recognizable names today from the Middle Ages, and his most famous work, *The Canterbury Tales*, is still taught in schools today. It provides a deep look at the types of lives and professions of the Middle Ages (and a view into how those kinds of people were viewed by the general populace) as a highly entertaining series of stories. His narrative has been frequently mimicked over the centuries as people strive to achieve anything nearly as entertaining and universal as the themes in his book. His descriptions are vivid and relatable, with memorable characters that could spawn their own biographies and works of fiction because of the amount of personality he puts into each of them. Some of his other works are also studied, but none have quite the same level of character development and historical significance as this one. Chaucer himself worked for the English government, including working for Edward III, Richard II, and Henry IV, all vastly different types of rulers. However, this collection of stories is what has kept his name alive for centuries after his death in 1400.

Finally, one of the most influential stories in all of European history was penned during the Middle Ages, and its significance on every literary work since is well documented and impossible to overstate—*The Divine Comedy* by Dante Alighieri (1265-1321). Most people have heard of the *Inferno*, the first third, called a canto, of this tale, and nearly everyone in the west is familiar with the name Dante. Both the *Inferno* and Dante himself are still referenced in movies, books, TV shows, and video games. The tale has permeated Western tradition in large part because it was a very biased take on Greek and Roman history, politics of his day, and how he thought historical figures and current figures would fare after death. He takes the readers on essentially a tour of the three realms of the Christian afterlife—Hell, Purgatory, and Heaven—and he is accompanied by a different guide through each of them. While the trips through Purgatory (covered in the second canto called *Purgatorio*) and Heaven (covered in the third canto called *Paradiso*) are more muted, the tour through the *Inferno* sparks the imagination and is incredibly amusing, even to people today. Some of the most quoted lines in Western literature come from this poem, with "Abandon all hope ye who enter here" (the sign over the gate to Hell) perhaps being the most famous. It is an absolutely inspired work that is still worth a read today because many of the historical figures are still well known today (such as Ulysses, Judas, and Virgil).

Chapter 12 – The Renaissance

When people discuss the Renaissance, they generally mean the Italian Renaissance, but it actually refers to the multiple phases of change that occurred over all of Europe. Each nation had its own period of transition from the Middle Ages to the early modern era. The Renaissance is largely considered the turning point that marked the final end of the Middle Ages, but there is no one defining event that officially ended it. There are arguments that say there were about 100 years of transition from the Middle Ages to the early modern era, but by the time the Renaissance was over, the Middle Ages had definitely ended.

One of the reasons that the Renaissance marks a definitive shift in eras is that the focus and thought processes began to significantly change. The Middle Ages emphasized the importance of Christianity, particularly the Roman Catholic teachings. By the time of the Renaissance, power had become consolidated and the corrupt nature of the Church was obvious. During the Renaissance and the following centuries, the power of the Church steadily declined as it fought against the brilliant scientists and philosophers of the time.

Prelude to the Renaissance

Science may not have been as important as theology during the Middle Ages, but it was a period that saw some world-changing inventions, particularly toward the end. Many of these inventions made the Renaissance possible. Although the Great Famine and the Black Death significantly reduced the population, by the beginning of the Renaissance, the population across much of Europe was growing again. Significant improvements in farming made it easier and faster to produce food, meaning that changes in the climate were less devasting than they had been. Quarantines had proven to be an effective way of preventing further spread of the plague in major cities and towns.

The improvements in agriculture and a better understanding of how to manage disease outbreaks made survival much easier. However, it was Johannes Gutenberg's printing press that allowed for significant advances in thinking and ideology. Books could not only be mass produced, but they could be sold for considerably less. This made reading more accessible as the growing population moved away from an agrarian economy into the cities.

All of these events contributed to the explosion of thoughts and ideas that have come to be known as the Renaissance.

Italian Renaissance

The change in thinking began in little pockets of Europe, but the first major shift occurred in Italy around 1480 and lasted until about 1520. There were many reasons why the first Renaissance took place in Italy. As the home to the head of the Roman Catholic Church, the country attracted many great minds from around the world. A number of prestigious universities had emerged by the time of the Renaissance in Italy, attracting even more people from around the continent.

With many major port cities, Italy also attracted ideas and great thinkers from many regions beyond Europe. Some of the most significant people to arrive came from the crumbling Byzantine Empire. Though Constantinople would not fall until 1453, people had been leaving the empire before the final battle. They brought with them the ideas and culture that had been preserved after the fall of Rome, reviving the ideas in the minds of Western Europeans. Although they were not the only influence, their arrival around the time of the Renaissance cannot be dismissed as a coincidence either.

Men like Leonardo da Vinci and Galileo Galilei learned to balance their investigations into the world around them with the paranoia of the Catholic Church. By working within the system, they were able to postulate ideas with less risk. They studied everything from biology and physics to nature and art to classical philosophy. Religion was not their main motivation, which was a significant departure from previous centuries. They did not want to dismiss religion, but they also did not want to be hindered by it. By establishing a delicate balance, they were able to explore ideas that were heretical to the Church. They were not immune from the anger of the Church, however (Galileo spent a number of years under house arrest toward the end of his life), but they understood the limits better than others, such as Giordano Bruno.

Renaissance thinking began to analyze more than just the sciences, too. Architects during the Renaissance didn't exactly reject the architecture of the Middle Ages, but they did seek a more classical appearance in their buildings, giving rise to beautiful and elaborate structures that were nearly as impressive as those of Rome. The ideas of Rome were considered paramount, and they sought to further those ideas over the philosophies and works of the Middle Ages.

At some point during the Renaissance, people tried to differentiate the obviously changing times. They used the term Renaissance to indicate the rebirth of thinking and ideas. Really, it was the return to a previous era, but they were more interested in painting the previous centuries as unenlightened. The idea that the time before the Renaissance was a dark period certainly has a basis in fact, given how much bloodshed occurred, but that kind of barbarity intensified after the Renaissance, with the most recent examples being both of the World Wars. The Renaissance was more of a significant shift in thinking than a rebirth, but it did place a new emphasis on science and progress, which had been far less important during the Middle Ages.

The Renaissance Spreads

Italy was the first country to experience a significant shift in thinking, but they were not the only country that began to reevaluate their way of thinking after the horrors and uncertainty of the Black Death and so many wars. Both France and England experienced significant changes during the 16th century, including changes in their politics and art. William Shakespeare is probably the most famous figure from this time, but there were many others who left their mark on their countries as the world began to move away from the authority of the Catholic Church.

In areas north of Italy, the Northern Renaissance saw changes in the Protestant regions. These ideas spread to the Americas, influencing the thought processes and beliefs in the colonies.

The Renaissance Fades

Historians do not agree on when the Renaissance ended. Some place the end around 1520 when the enthusiasm and major players of the Italian Renaissance were gone. Others place the end of the era around 1620 when the spirit of renewal and ideas died down across the continent.

What is indisputable is that Western thinking never returned back to the blind faith that many had in their religion, which was the mindset of the Middle Ages. As more people became educated, ideas were more easily evolved and spread. Following the Renaissance, Europe experienced a steady shift into more scientific thinking and away from the mysticism of religion. Following the Renaissance was the Enlightenment, which ended with several revolutions and a considerable amount of bloodshed. World-altering inventions came along far more frequently and were not always fully understood before they showed their devasting effects (such as the machines of the Industrial Revolution that significantly polluted the environment and poisoned people in cities).

With people more inclined to turn to science to find the causes of problems, fewer people believed it was simply the will of an omnipotent being they could not understand. Science became far more important and resulted in both astonishing and horrific creations that still continue today.

Conclusion

The Middle Ages is an often misunderstood period of European history. Beginning after the fall of Rome and its grip on Western Europe, the Middle Ages marked a tumultuous time that saw religion playing an increasingly significant role in the lives of everyone. Christianity changed between the fall of Rome and the Renaissance, and much of the period reflects the changes in the Church.

After people were no longer tied to the Roman Empire, men began to seek power and nations began to form under the strongest leaders. Some of Europe's most notable leaders lived during this period, including Charlemagne, who briefly united many regions of the former Roman Empire under his banner. This proved to be unsustainable by those who followed him though, and the continent again fell under the control of different tribes and factions. By the end of the Middle Ages, you can begin to see the outline of the current map of Europe.

The fall of Rome did not mark the end of the empire, or at least not the end of the progress that they had made. It simply shifted the location from Rome to Constantinople. The rise of the Byzantine Empire ensured that much of the research, literature, art, and works of the Roman period were preserved and carried forward by the people within the new empire. A few of the emperors tried to retake the former parts of the Roman Empire in the west, but they were mostly unsuccessful. The majority of the Christian world fell under their empire as well, something that increasingly became a point of contention with the rising power in Rome. Originally part of the sister churches of the Byzantine Empire, the pope in Rome ended up being removed, and within a century, two entirely different Christian churches formed after the Great Schism.

War was incredibly common during this time, as the Romans had trained many of the Germanic tribes that had been absorbed into the Roman Empire. These tactics were turned on each other as leaders rose and fell. Perhaps the most tragic of these was the 200 years when the Christian people were taught to believe that they needed to go kill people in the name of Jesus so that they could reclaim his land. The Crusades not only took advantage of the faith of the knights, peasants, and other devout followers, but it also warped the Church. After the last Crusade, the Church emerged as the dominant power across the continent. It ruled with a cruel fist that did not allow for dissent or even questioning. Science became increasingly risky, even during the Renaissance, and people could be claimed as being heretical for contradicting or even questioning the Church's teachings of pseudo-science. The various Crusades were the first major abuse of the Church, and they were largely brought about by powerful people looking for personal gain.

As the Hundred Years' War proved, religion was not the only perpetrator of prolonged fighting and bloodshed. The war between France and England carried on for close to 120 years because of the desire of the kings and their nobles to have their own king on the throne of France. It was the peasants, serfs, and those who lived in towns that suffered the most as knights and mercenaries pillaged and looted places even during years of relative peace. From this lowly class came one of the most famous peasants of the Middle Ages, Joan of Arc. She turned the tides against the English, even if her victories were limited to the first few attacks that she led. Because of her determination and abilities, the French were able to finally retake the areas that the English claimed, and the English never fully recovered. The war ended, but that did not stop the fighting in either country. England began a civil war that came to be known as the War of the Roses (referring to the white and red roses that represented the two houses fighting for the throne). France turned its attention to other wars as they had enemies both in Spain and the Holy Roman Empire.

These events were not the only defining characteristics of the period though, as much as people tend to think of them that way. The Middle Ages also saw some of the most staggering architectural achievements in the form of Gothic architecture, with buildings that are still standing today. This architecture has proven to be inspiring for artists of all mediums but most notably in literature and modern movies. Mary Shelley was one of the first to use this impressive architecture in her works, and it has become closely linked to the horror and mystery genres.

While later centuries would see a movement to romanticize the time before the Renaissance, even the people of the Renaissance used some of the ideas and concepts from the previous era. Many of the ideas of the Renaissance had some of their foundations in the Middle Ages, not just in classical Roman ideas. Even today, the works of Thomas Aquinas and Dante are so integral that they are referenced almost without any kind of thought today.

There were many tragedies, including the Great Famine, the Hundred Years' War, the Crusades, and the Black Death, but they were not the only events that define the time between the 6th century and the 14th or 15th centuries. By looking around Europe today, one can see the residual influence of the Middle Ages in their structures, art, and literature. So many things that are taken granted for today actually had their roots during this period of transition. Consider how devastated people were across the world at the news that the Notre Dame Cathedral might be lost. Imagine how different literature and entertainment would be today without some of the core literary works that defined Europe during this period. The Middle Ages were about much more than death and war; it was a time of growth and development after the fall of Rome, a city that had ruled so much of Europe for centuries. Peoples and regions that had little in common were able to develop their own identities and political structures. In its own way, it was a rebirth, just into a chaotic world, compared to the Renaissance which was a rebirth from the rigid structures of the Church.

Here's another book by Captivating History you might like

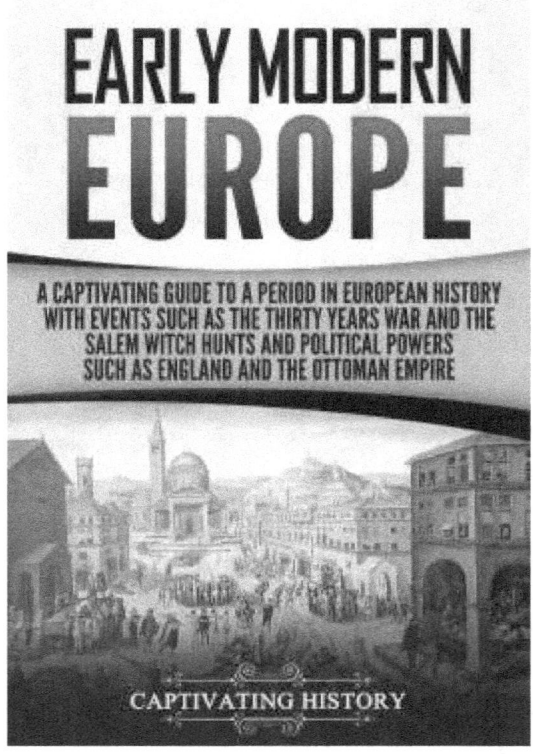

Free Bonus from Captivating History (Available for a Limited time)

Hi History Lovers!

Now you have a chance to join our exclusive history list so you can get your first history ebook for free as well as discounts and a potential to get more history books for free! Simply visit the link below to join.

Captivatinghistory.com/ebook

Also, make sure to follow us on Facebook, Twitter and Youtube by searching for Captivating History.

Bibliography

#203 Life of Charlemagne: 2019, Christian History Institute, christianhistoryinstitute.org

1204: The Sack of Constantinople: Mark Cartwright, February 1, 2018, Ancient History Encyclopedia, www.ancient.edu

1215 the Year of Magna Carta: Danny Danziger and John Gillingham, Touchstone Book, 2003-2005, New York, USA

A Beginner's Guide to the Renaissance: Robert Wilde, April 15, 2018, ThoughtCo, www.thoughtco.com

AD 732, Battle of Tours: Charles Martel the "Hammer" Holds the Line of Battle: William McLaughlin, February 25 2018, War History Online, www.warhistoryonline.com

Battle of Hastings: The Editors of Encyclopedia Britannica, February 4, 2019, Encyclopedia Britannica Inc, www.britannica.com

Byzantine Conference: Famous Emperors: Famous Emperors, March 13, 2019, http://www.byzconf.org

Byzantine Empire: Historical Empire, Eurasia: John L. Terall, February 8, 2019, Encyclopedia Britannica, www.britannica.com

Byzantine Empire: Mark Cartwright, September 19, 2018, Ancient History Encyclopedia, www.ancient.eu/Byzantine_Empire/

Canterbury Tales, Geoffrey Chaucer, Alfred A. Knope Inc., 1958.

Charlemagne: 2014, BBC, http://www.bbc.co.uk

Charles Martel: Eleanor Shipley Duckett, January 11, 2019, Encyclopedia Britannia, www.britannica.com

Crusades Timeline: 2019, m.datesandevents.org

Crusades: Christianity: Gary Dickson, Thomas F., Madden, Marshall Baldwin, October 26 2018, Encyclopedia Britannica Inc, www.britannica.com

Dante: Siteseen Ltd., March 2018, www.medieval-life-and-times.info

Edward III (1312 – 1377): BBC, 2014, www.bbc.co

Edward, the Black Prince (1330 -1376): BBC, 2014, www.bbc.co

Edward: King of England [1002?-1066]: The Editors of Encyclopedia Britannica, January 1 2019, Encyclopedia Britannica Inc, www.britannica.com

Eleanor of Aquitaine (c.1122 – 1204): BBC, 2014, www.bbc.co

Eleventh Century: The Great Schism: The Orthodox Church in America, 1996-2019, oca.org

Empress Matilda (Maud) 1102 – 1167: Heather Y Wheeler. (2015). Empress Matilda (Maud) 1102 – 1167. Available: https://www.totallytimelines.com/empress-matilda-maud-1102-1167

Empress Maud: Ben Johnson, 2019, Historic UK Ltd, www.historic-uk.com

Fall of Rome: How, When, Why Did It Happen: N.S. Gill, January 14, 2019, ThoughtCo, www.thoughtco.com/

Fall of the western Roman Empire: Donald L. Wasson, April 12, 2018, Ancient History Encyclopedia Limited, www.ancient.eu

Geoffrey Chaucer: R.M Lumiansky, October 21, 2018, Encyclopedia Britannia, www.britannica.com

Gothic Architecture: Siteseen Ltd., March 2018, www.medieval-life-and-times.info

Gothic Architecture: Victoria and Albert Museum, 2016, www.vam.ac.uk

Hardecanute: King of Denmark and England: The Editors of Encyclopedia Britannica, June 4 2018, Encyclopedia Britannica Inc, www.britannica.com

History: The Fall of Rome: Dr Peter Hether, February 17 2011, BBC, www.bbc.co.uk

Holy Roman Emperor Otto I: Melissa Snell, February 16, 2019, Though Co, Dotdash Publishing, www.thoughtco.com

How Joan of Arc Turned the Tide in the Hundred Years War: Julien Thèry, March 2017, National Geographic, www.nationalgeographic.com

Leo III Attacked in a Procession: Dan Graves, 2019, JupiterImages Co, www.christianity.com

Lost to the West: Lars Brownworth, 2009, Random House Inc, New York

Marco Polo: Siteseen Ltd., March 2018, www.medieval-life-and-times.info

Origin of the Magna Carta: Doris Mary Stenton, September 21, 2018, Encyclopedia Britannica Inc, www.britannica.com

Otto 1: Medieval Chronicles, 2014-2019, www.medievalchronicles.com

Otto I: Encyclopedia of World Biography, 2004, The Gale Group Inc.

Rise & Fall of the Roman, Ottoman & Byzantine Empires: Christopher Muscato, 2003-2019, study.com

Sailing from Byzantium: How a Lost Empire Shaped the World: Colin Wells, 2006, Bantam Dell, New York, USA

The Crusades: Causes & Goals: Mark Cartwright, July 4 2018, Ancient History Encyclopedia, www.ancient.edu

The Great Crusades (1095-1291): Erbstösser, Hallam, Riley Smith, 2019, www.umich.edu

The Great Famine (1315-1317) and the Black Death (1346-1351): Lynn Harry Nelson, 2019, Lecture in Medieval History, www.vib.us

The Great Schism Explained: Tony Wesolowsky, February 5, 2016, RadioFreeEurope RadioLiberty, www.rferl.org/

The Great Schism of 1054: Boundless World History. Authored by: Boundless. Located at: https://www.boundless.com/world-history/textbooks/boundless-world-history-textbook/.

The Great Schism: 2019, greatschism.org

The Hundred Years War: Robert Wilde, March 22, 2019, Thought Co, www.thoughtco.com

The Hundred Years' War, 1336 – 1453: Lynn Harry Nelson, 2019, Lecture in Medieval History, www.vib.us

The Later Roman Empire: Averil Cameron, 1993, USA

Thomas Aquinas (1224/6 – 1274): Christopher M. Brown, 2019, Internet Encyclopedia of Philosophy, www.iep.utm.edu/aquinas/

Timeline of Major Events of the Crusades: The Sultan and the Saint, 2015-2019, Unity Productions Foundation, www.sultanandthesaintfilm.com

Universities – the Beginning of Higher Education: Master and More, 2019, www.master-and-more.eu

What Is Magna Carta?: Terry Jones, 2019, British Library

Who's Really the Last Roman Emperor?: Ken Lohatenpanot, August 17, 2013, History Republic, historyrepublic.wordpress.com

www.ingramcontent.com/pod-product-compliance
Lightning Source LLC
LaVergne TN
LVHW012121070526
838202LV00056B/5818